Legends of the Wild West

Geronimo

Legends of the Wild West

Sitting Bull

Billy the Kid

Calamity Jane

Buffalo Bill Cody

Crazy Horse

Davy Crockett

Wyatt Earp

Geronimo

Wild Bill Hickok

Jesse James

Nat Love

Annie Oakley

Legends of the Wild West

Geronimo

South Huntington Pub. Lib.
145 Pidgeon Hill Rd.
Huntington Sta., N.Y. 11746

Jon Sterngass

Geronimo
Copyright © 2010 by Infobase Publishing

All rights reserved. No part of this book may be reproduced or utilized in any form or by any means, electronic or mechanical, including photocopying, recording, or by any information storage or retrieval systems, without permission in writing from the publisher. For information, contact:

Chelsea House
An imprint of Infobase Publishing
132 West 31st Street
New York NY 10001

Library of Congress Cataloging-in-Publication Data
Sterngass, Jon.
  Geronimo / Jon Sterngass.
    p. cm. — (Legends of the Wild West)
  Includes bibliographical references and index.
  ISBN 978-1-60413-525-1 (hardcover)
  1. Geronimo, 1829-1909—Juvenile literature. 2. Apache Indians—Kings and rulers—Biography—Juvenile literature. 3. Apache Indians—Wars—Juvenile literature. I. Title. II. Series.
  E99.A6G32743 2010
  970.004'97—dc22
  [B]   2010006597

Chelsea House books are available at special discounts when purchased in bulk quantities for businesses, associations, institutions, or sales promotions. Please call our Special Sales Department in New York at (212) 967-8800 or (800) 322-8755.

You can find Chelsea House on the World Wide Web at
http://www.chelseahouse.com

Text design by Kerry Casey
Cover design by Keith Trego
Composition by EJB Publishing Services
Cover printed by Bang Printing, Brainerd, Minn.
Book printed and bound by Bang Printing, Brainerd, Minn.
Date printed: August 2010
Printed in the United States of America

10 9 8 7 6 5 4 3 2 1

This book is printed on acid-free paper.

All links and Web addresses were checked and verified to be correct at the time of publication. Because of the dynamic nature of the Web, some addresses and links may have changed since publication and may no longer be valid.

CONTENTS

1	Resolution 132	7
2	Goyathlay's Youth	13
3	"I Had Lost All"	25
4	Enter the Americans	36
5	San Carlos	51
6	Renegade	65
7	The Last Breakout	76
8	Living Legend	88
9	Healing Old Wounds	101

Chronology	108
Timeline	108
Glossary	113
Bibliography	116
Further Resources	120
Picture Credits	123
Index	124
About the Author	128

RESOLUTION 132

The year 2009 was the one hundredth anniversary of Geronimo's death. In his honor, the U.S. House of Representatives passed Congressional Resolution 132. In this resolution, Congress stated that it officially

> (1) Honors the life of Goyathlay, also known as Geronimo, his extraordinary bravery, and his commitment to the defense of his homeland, his people, and Apache ways of life; and
>
> (2) Recognizes the 100th anniversary of the death of Goyathlay as a time of reflection of his deeds on behalf of his people.

No one would have been more surprised by this honor than Geronimo, the war leader and shaman (spiritual leader) of the Chiricahua Apaches. For when he died in 1909, he was the very symbol of the bloodthirsty American Indian to most white people. A *New York Times* obituary summarized his life: "Geronimo gained a reputation for cruelty and cunning never surpassed by that of any other American Indian chief. For more than twenty years, he and his men were the terror of the country, always leaving a trail of bloodshed and devastation." Yet over the last century, Geronimo's reputation

In the 1800s, Apache leader Geronimo was seen by his supporters as a proud symbol of resistance and the upholder of the Chiricahua ways. To others, especially white settlers, he was a troublemaker and a cold-blooded killer. Today, Geronimo is an enduring figure of the now-tamed Wild West.

has moved from the whites' most hated foe to a romanticized symbol of Native American resistance.

Even after 100 years, it is still hard to capture Geronimo's nature. He has become all things to all people. To try to describe him is to reveal the elusiveness of historical truth. He was a hero and a villain, a murderer and a freedom fighter, a terrorist and a brilliant military strategist, a wise philosopher and a childlike clown. He was honest and deceitful, hard working and lazy, a drunkard and an ascetic. He made a virtual religion of unrelenting revenge against Mexicans, and he fought Americans long past hope and reason. Resolution 132 called him "a spiritual and intellectual leader who led his people in a war of self-defense," yet he also killed women and children in cold blood.

HISTORY IS ABOUT INTERPRETATION, NOT FACTS

Many people want history to be about facts. They memorize that Geronimo surrendered to General Miles in 1886 and died in 1909. That is true but does not really mean much. There are trillions and trillions of "facts" like these. It is how they are put together and interpreted that makes history. It depends which facts are chosen and which are discarded. It depends on whom the interpreter is and what he or she hopes to show. A biography of Geronimo from the Apache point of view would look very different from the same biography written from the perspective of a white Arizona settler.

The story of Geronimo and the Apache Wars reveals the importance of interpretation in history. In 1886, whites considered him a cold-blooded murderer, the worst of the worst. As the years passed, Geronimo began to symbolize the heroic fight of a brave people for independence and ownership of their traditional homeland. Articles praised him as a courageous fighter and a superb tactician. Novels, movies, and television portrayed Geronimo in a sympathetic light. The "facts" did not change; it was the way that people put the facts together that changed.

During World War II, paratroopers from the 501st Parachute Infantry Regiment began using the cry "Geronimo" when they jumped from an airplane. According to legend, the night before their first mass jump, U.S. paratroopers watched the movie *Geronimo*. The 1939 film portrayed Geronimo as a bloodthirsty villain whose only pleasure was slaughtering whites, preferably defenseless women and children. In one scene, Geronimo yells his name as he leaps from a high cliff into a river. The members of the 501st Parachute Infantry Regiment began to imitate the scene when they jumped from airplanes. Soon, the regiment's motto and slogan were named after Geronimo.

The phrase "Geronimo" became closely tied to paratroopers and then parachutists in general. Then it became widely associated in popular culture with any kind of high jump or attack. The expression further popularized the Apache war leader and enhanced his reputation. From there, it was only a small step to appearing in Congressional Resolution 132: "Whereas Goyathlay's byname, 'Geronimo,' became a war cry uttered by paratroopers fighting against the totalitarian enemies of the United States during World War II, a name used with respect and honor for a great warrior and leader..."

A SYMBOL OF RESISTANCE

Geronimo is at his best when viewed as a symbol of resistance. He was born in the mid-1820s in what is today western New Mexico. He was a member of the Apache, a nomadic tribe that lived by raising some food, hunting and gathering, and raiding their neighbors. The Apache were a warrior society, and Geronimo was a successful organizer and leader of war parties. He was also recognized as a medicine man with supernatural powers. Many fellow tribesmen respected and feared him.

Unfortunately for the Apache, Americans invaded their lands in the 1850s. The futile but strong resistance of the Apache brought national fame to several of their leaders, such as Mangas Coloradas, Cochise, Victorio, Nana, and finally, Geronimo. By the mid-1880s, the U.S. Army had forced most of the Apache bands on to

In 1940, the word *Geronimo* became a motto and slogan of the 501st Parachute Infantry Regiment. After viewing the film *Geronimo*, in which a character yells the legendary Apache's name while leaping from a cliff, a U.S. private announced he would shout the name when he jumped from a plane to prove he was not scared. Today, shouting "Geronimo" when attempting a high jump has become part of popular culture.

reservations. Geronimo, with a handful of fellow raiders, held out until finally surrendering in 1886. His surrender was the last significant Native American guerrilla action in the United States (although the massacre of the Sioux at Wounded Knee, South Dakota, occurred in 1890).

Because Geronimo fought against such daunting odds and because he held out the longest, he became the most famous Apache of all. In a sense, this is peculiar because he does not fit an easy niche in historical memory. Geronimo is not associated with one major battle like Sitting Bull and Crazy Horse (Little Big Horn). He is not associated with a heroic and epic retreat like Chief Joseph of the Nez Perce or Little Wolf of the Cheyenne.

In fact, Geronimo did not primarily concern himself with Americans. He did most of his fiercest fighting against Mexicans, whom he despised with an undying hatred after they killed his wife and family. The wars between the U.S. government and the Apache lasted barely 25 years. This pales in comparison with the 250 years that the Apache fought the Spanish and the Mexicans. Yet in the end, it would be the Americans who ended the Apache's nomadic lifestyle.

Geronimo was not defeated in battle. Even as a prisoner of war for 23 years, he struggled mightily to maintain his dignity and help his people. He constantly displayed heroism against overwhelming odds. Geronimo's energy, determination, and sturdy independence distinguished him throughout his life. These qualities made him a leader of the Apache. They have enabled his reputation to survive, despite his flaws, as a "great American."

GOYATHLAY'S YOUTH

Goyathlay (henceforth referred to as Geronimo) was born to the Bedonkohe band of the Chiricahua Apache near Turkey Creek, a tributary of the Gila River. The exact site was probably in the modern-day state of New Mexico, north of Silver City. At the time, the land was part of Mexico but Geronimo's family considered it Bedonkohe land. Despite the certainty of the date in the Congressional Resolution (a date taken from Geronimo's autobiography), Geronimo's actual birth year is unknown; sometime in the mid-1820s seems to be the best guess.

Goyathlay means "One Who Yawns," but the significance of the name or the way he received it is not known. Geronimo's father, Taklishim, was the son of Mahko, a great Bedonkohe leader. His mother's name was Juana, a Spanish name. It serves as a reminder how the Southwest's Hispanic and Apache populations had become interconnected over the centuries through raiding, trading, and enslavement. Geronimo later said he had three brothers and four sisters but as far as is known, all but one of those were cousins. There is no word in the Apache language to distinguish cousins from siblings.

In old age, Geronimo still remembered his first years of life. He recalled rolling on the earth floor of his father's lodge and hanging in a cradle from his mother's back. He said, "I was warmed by the sun, rocked by the winds, and sheltered by the trees as other Indian babes."

Juana educated him according to Apache traditions. Geronimo recalled that, "When a child my mother taught me the legends of our people; taught me of the sun and the sky, the moon and stars, the clouds and storms." He grew up with the traditional religious views of the Apache. As a child, Geronimo learned to pray to Ussen, a remote Supreme Being (or Life Force) sometimes called "Life Giver."

Apache society taught children that they must endure suffering without complaint. A child old enough to walk and talk rarely cried. However, there were also happy times when Geronimo played hide and seek among the rocks and pines with his playmates. The children pretended to be warriors stalking a make-believe enemy. His father told him stories of the "brave deeds of our warriors, of the pleasures of the chase, and of the glories of the warpath."

Geronimo and his age-mates grew up in a time of peace, a rare condition in Apache history. He later said, "During my minority we had never seen a missionary or a priest. We had never seen a white man. Thus quietly lived the Bedonkohe Apaches."

Taklishim died when Geronimo was a young man. Juana never remarried, although, as Geronimo noted, "according to the customs of our tribe she might have done so immediately after his death." Instead, she chose to live with her young son. "We lived near our old home and I supported her," he recalled.

When Geronimo was about 17, he arranged to wed a girl named Alope, a member of another Chiricahua band called the Nednhi. "She was a slender, delicate girl," he recalled, "but we had been lovers for a long time." Alope's father asked for many ponies before Geronimo could wed his daughter, but this did not stop the young man. In a few days, he appeared before Alope's father with a herd of horses. Then he rode off with his new bride. He did not think it necessary to explain how he acquired the horses or whether he had killed anyone in getting them.

"This was all the marriage ceremony necessary in our tribe," he stated. As another Apache noted, "Marriage is something in the heart, not words mumbled by some Medicine Man."

APACHERÍA

The Apache lived mainly in present-day southeastern Arizona and southwestern New Mexico. However, their raiding and trading trips took them deep into the Mexican provinces of Sonora and Chihuahua (just across the border from present-day Arizona, New Mexico, and Texas). This entire "four-state" region totaled several thousand square miles and was known as Apachería. Throughout the 1800s, Hispanics, Anglos, and other Apache groups shared and fought over the land. By the time Geronimo was born, the Apache had lived in the area for several centuries

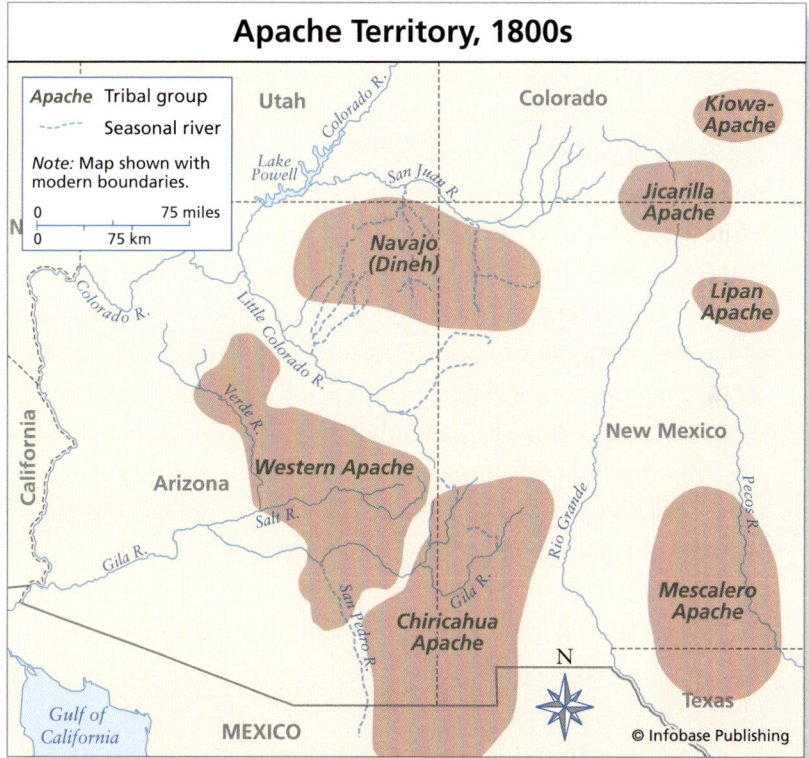

The Apache lived in nomadic bands and controlled much of the Southwest before the arrival of white settlers. The Navajo, who were linguistically related to the Apache, also lived in the Southwest. This map shows the territory claimed by the Navajo and by the different bands of Apache during the 1800s.

and knew Apachería's mesas, canyons, mountain ranges, rivers, and deserts quite well.

Apache peoples might now be called "Native Americans" but they were not at all native to the Southwest. Centuries ago, their ancestors lived as far north as Canada. Somewhere between A.D. 1000 and 1300, some people of this group began an extended migration to the south. They probably arrived in the Southwest during the 1500s, not long before the Spanish arrived. Compared to the Pueblo, Pima, and Yuma peoples of the Southwest, the Apache are newcomers to the area.

Somewhere in their long journey to the Southwest, the Apache subdivided into groups that might be called "tribes." Some of the larger groups are known as the Jicarilla, Kiowa, Lipan, Chiricahua, Mescalero, and Western Navajo. Each of these tribes, united by a similar language, occupied a different region of the Southwest.

When the Apache peoples moved into the Southwest, they lived by hunting and gathering small game and wild plants. In the Apache people's new environment, two groups split almost completely apart from the Apache. The eastern Kiowa Apache became buffalo hunters, lived in Plains-type teepees, and shared the history of the Kiowa. Another Apachean group, the Navajo, chose a different path. They became raisers of sheep, and the Apache regarded them as a separate tribe with a completely different culture. The remaining Apache had nothing but contempt for raising sheep.

It is almost impossible to untangle completely the tribal divisions of the Apache. The groups were not tribes in the stereotypical way. The Apache lived in nomadic subgroups of between 30 and 200 people. Within these societies, there were further subdivisions, each with a recognized leader or chief.

HUNTING AND FIGHTING

Geronimo made a new lodge near the one for his mother. The family lived happily. He and Alope "followed the traditions of our fathers and were happy. Three children came to us," Geronimo recalled, "children that played, loitered, and worked as I had done."

Goyathlay's Youth   17

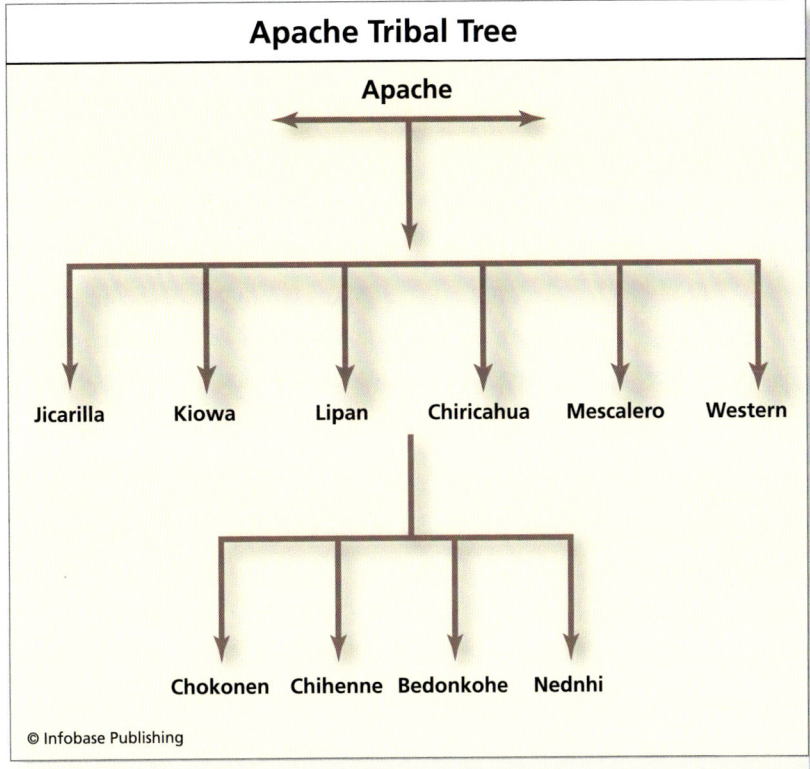

The Apache Indians were a powerful group who were constantly at odds with Anglos and Mexicans. The Apache subdivided into six groups who had little political unity and spoke six different languages. Although the Navajo and the Apache groups have a similar culture and language indicating they were once a single ethnic group, the Navajo are not considered a branch of the modern Apache.

Life in Apachería was hard but pleasant. Geronimo remembered, "Among these mountains our wigwams were hidden; the scattered valleys contained our fields; the boundless prairies, stretching away on every side, were our pastures; the rocky caverns were our burying places."

The young Geronimo particularly enjoyed hunting. The Bedonkohe hunted mule deer, elk, antelope, and turkey. Geronimo considered deer to be the most difficult prey to kill. Sometimes, he said, Apache hunters "would spend hours in stealing upon grazing deer. If they were in the open, we would crawl long distances on the ground, keeping a weed or brush before us, so that our approach would not be noticed." After a successful kill, the deer meat would be dried and stored for several months and the skins tanned to make them soft enough for making articles of clothing. "Perhaps no other animal," Geronimo explained, "was more valuable to us than the deer."

The skills that Geronimo learned as a young hunter would also be superb training for the life of a warrior. Apache boys were carefully trained for war; they were taught to endure pain and to inflict it. They learned how to shoot a gun and bow and arrow, hide in various types of environments, track animals and humans, map the terrain, and find their way back to camp. The Apache had many contests for men and boys to practice these skills, such as arrow shooting, racing, and wrestling. Excited betting took place on all these games, for the Apache were famous as chronic gamblers.

Young Apache boys helped to care for horses and learned to make weapons and tools. But to become a warrior, a young Apache boy had to go through a strict period as an apprentice to an older man. Geronimo's cousin, Jason Betzinez, explained that the "way to learn was to go on several raids with an experienced man, taking care of his horses and equipment, standing guard, and cooking his meat for him. That was the Apache custom." Betzinez earned his own warrior status by serving as Geronimo's apprentice.

APACHE LIFE

The Apache loved the wild jumble of canyons and mountains that made up their Southwestern homeland. Geronimo once said that when "Ussen created the Apaches, He also created their homes in the West. He gave them such grain, fruits, and game as they needed to eat.... He gave them a pleasant climate and all they needed for clothing and shelter was at hand." The Apache knew the uses of every plant and the habits of every animal. At the end of his life, Geronimo said, "There is no climate or soil which, to my mind, is equal to that of Arizona."

Goyathlay's Youth

A wickiup was used by many different Native American cultures. They varied in size, shape, and materials, and the woman was responsible for its construction and maintenance. Pictured is a wickiup outside the Apache Cultural Center at the Fort Apache Indian Reservation in Arizona.

The western Apache sometimes lived in teepees but usually in brush shelters, known as wickiups, that a family could build in half a day. The Apache constructed a wickiup by inserting many slender poles in the ground, making a circle about 12 feet (144 inches) in diameter. They brought the poles almost together at the top, covered with grass or brush, and then with another layer of deerskins or blankets. The fire would be made in the center of the wickiup and the smoke ventilated out the top. When an Apache died, his wickiup and all his possessions were burned or buried with him or her.

Most Apache groups raised a few crops such as squash, beans, and corn on small, secluded fields. They collected wild medicinal herbs and a variety of tobacco. The Apache also hunted wild game and gathered piñon nuts, juniper berries, prickly pear fruit, yucca fruit, and the seeds of wild shrubs and grass. Their most important food was mescal—the heart of certain kinds of agave plants. In late spring, the women would dig up these plants and sun-bake the hearts. Sun-dried, baked mescal was a vital Apache foodstuff, carried with the tribe through the rest of the year. "The Apaches are born and reared in the open air of the country," wrote a Spanish army officer, "and fortified by simple foods, are possessed of amazing hardiness."

The Apache peoples also used their corn to make a fermented drink known as tizwin. Geronimo noted that tizwin "had the power of intoxication, and was very highly prized" by the Apache. It had a relatively low alcoholic counter and spoiled quickly, so the Apache would make it in large batches and drink it quickly, in vast quantities at feasts. Often these drunken bashes would lead to violence and throw the whole tribe into disorder.

The Apache were migratory nomads who hunted and farmed according to the seasons. Less than half of the food they ate in a year came from agricultural products; the rest came from wild plants, game animals, and stolen livestock. Unable to rely on a surplus of crops, the Apache traveled widely in search of food. For this reason, they did not establish permanent residences in any one spot. Except in winter, when plant-gathering activities came to a virtual standstill, they were almost constantly on the move.

Despite their migratory culture, the Apache had a rich ceremonial and cultural life. The most important ceremony in Apache life was probably the girls' puberty ritual, which lasted through four days and nights of dancing.

APACHE RAIDING

The Apache are famous for their fierce fighting qualities. For several centuries, they successfully resisted the advance of Spanish colonization in northern Mexico, despite the fact that they never numbered more than a few thousand people. The coming of the Spanish gave the Apache horses for the first time. Once they learned to ride, they began raiding settled Pueblo and Navajo colonies and even other Apache groups.

Sometime in the late 1600s, the Apache extended their raiding to Mexican villages and ranches in Sonora and along the Rio Grande. By 1800, Apache life depended on the livestock and other plunder stolen from Mexican ranchers and native farmers. The Apache did not even breed their own horses like the Navajo; instead, they stole the livestock when they needed it. The Apache got in the habit of raiding the Spanish villages at harvest time while ignoring them the rest of the year.

Raiding the settled communities became a way of life for the Apache. In Apache society, people considered raiding as legitimate an economic enterprise as gathering berries or hunting deer. Tribal leaders and warriors proved themselves on raids. Apache women greeted successful raiders with songs, rejoicing, and a victory dance. The Apache warriors had no great desire to kill Mexicans, for that would only bring trouble. Mostly, they wanted only to bring back enough supplies for the winter and their ceremonies.

In the 1700s, Spanish soldiers and militia fought back against the Apache. Spanish officials struggled—long, hard, and unsuccessfully—to end Apache raiding. Sometimes, the Spanish tried to exterminate the Apache by paying bounties for their scalps, ears, and heads. When the two groups fought, both sides expected rewards in the form of spoils. The winners took any livestock but also women and children who formed the basis of a slave trade important to Apache and Spanish life.

APACHE STRATEGY

The most terrifying thing about the Apache was their stealth. Their attacks seemed to come without any warning. Like most Native tribes, the Apache learned to avoid pitched battles when outnumbered. Geronimo himself said, "It is senseless to fight when you cannot hope to win." One U.S. Army officer said, "The Apache has no

The Apache Language

The Apache speak a language that has various dialects and belongs to the Athabascan branch of the Nadene language of the American Southwest. In the 1800s, it was common in Arizona, New Mexico, and Texas. It was a spoken language only with no written form.

In the late 1800s, the United States made organized attempts to eliminate the Apache language and replace it with English. At the famous Carlisle [PA] Indian School, the use of Native languages was strictly prohibited. These attempts at cultural genocide did not succeed. As of 2009, there are about 15,000 speakers of Apachean languages in the Southwest. For Apache parents, speaking the Apache language and teaching it to their children is one of the most important ways they try to keep their heritage.

Apache is a complicated language in which glottal stops and pitch carry meaning while vowels may be short or long and nasalized or not. Translation was a problem in all meetings between the Apache and Americans. Only a handful of whites in the 1800s, most notably George Wratten, ever learned more than a few Apache words.

---

false ideas about courage; he would prefer to skulk like the coyote for hours, and then kill his enemy, or capture his herd, rather than, by injudicious exposure, receive a wound, fatal or otherwise. But he is no coward; on the contrary, he is entitled to rank among the bravest."

Formal boasting of prowess in war, common among the Native tribes on the Plains, was frowned upon by the Apache as rude bragging. Tribes like the Sioux and the Cheyenne believed in counting coup to win prestige in battle. In Sioux culture, it was a great honor for a warrior to risk his life to be the first to touch an enemy warrior in battle and escape unharmed.

The Apache did not count coup; they thought the concept was incredibly foolish. General Crook's chief aide wrote, "The Apache ... knew his business and played his cards to suit himself. He never

Geronimo, like most Apache peoples, knew a little Spanish from his dealings with Mexicans. That meant that when dealing with Americans, the talk was interpreted from Apache into Spanish and from Spanish into English and then the reverse. Some major misunderstandings in Southwestern history were probably due to this process of faulty translation.

Sample text in Apache	Translation
'Iłk'ida, k QQ yá'édiná'a.	Long ago, there was no fire.
'Ákoo Tł'ízhe hooghéí dá'áíná bikQ''óliná'a.	Then only those who are called Flies had fire.
'Ákoo Tł'ízheí gotál yiis'aná'a.	Then the Flies held a ceremony.
'Ákoo Mai'áee hiłghoná'a.	And Coyote came there.
Gotál jiis'aí 'áee, Mai tsíbaaee naaná'azhishná'a.	At that place where they held the ceremony,
'Ákoo bitseeí tsínáiłgoná'a.	Coyote danced around and around at the edge of the fire.
	And he continually poked his tail in the fire.

lost a shot, and never lost a warrior in a fight where a brisk run across the nearest ridge would save his life and exhaust the heavily clad soldiers who endeavored to catch him...."

Over centuries of fighting with the Spanish, the Apache adapted a perfect style of guerrilla warfare. They could travel long distances very quickly without food and water. The Apache could see trails that no other human eye could see and knew the location of every water hole and hidden canyon. Men, women, and children traveled with incredible secrecy, even though they rarely traveled at night. They could strike their enemy here today and 100 miles (160 kilometers) away tomorrow.

The Apache preferred to travel and fight on foot. However, if they had horses, they rode. If the going got too rough, they killed and ate their mounts and continued on foot until they could steal more horses. If attacked, the Apache seemed to scatter and "melt into the surrounding rocks," as witnesses often reported. They traveled separately in order to leave no trail and reassembled at some predetermined place.

An Apache chief was obligated to lead his men into battle. Apache fighters had great contempt for the American and Mexican commanders who sent their men into battle and watched the fighting from a safe distance. Apache society was both individualistic and democratic, however. An Apache chief could never command his men to fight, only try to persuade them. Each warrior made his own decisions and leaders drew followers only as long as their decisions earned respect.

For this reason, Apache war parties were quite small. Probably no Apache war party in history exceeded 200 warriors, and the Apache never united to engage in formal warfare. To a degree, even this worked in their favor. It was almost impossible for their enemies to take decisive action against them. Apache warriors, though never numerous, were extremely capable and resourceful.

In general, an Apache could not be accepted into the "council of warriors" until he had accompanied the warriors four times. Geronimo said that he was accepted into the council at age 17. "I hoped soon to serve my people in battle," he remembered. "I had long desired to fight with our warriors."

"I HAD LOST ALL"

Geronimo's family may have been growing, but his life was no longer peaceful. In 1821, Mexico had won its independence from Spain. The Mexican government tried to assert its authority on the enormous and sparsely populated northern frontier by beginning a campaign of extermination. Between 1835 and the 1880s, the Mexican authorities hired private armies to hunt the Apache, paying them per kill and using scalps as receipts. The policy began in 1835 and 1837 when the northern Mexican states of Sonora and Chihuahua placed a bounty on Apache scalps: $100 for men, $50 for women, and $25 for children.

At about this time, Mangas Coloradas became the principal chief and war leader of the Apache of southwest New Mexico. Trappers massacred many of Mangas's band in 1837 in order to receive the bounty for Apache scalps. In the 1840s, the Apache under Mangas began a series of brutal retaliatory raids against the Mexicans in Sonora. Numerous atrocities by each side caused even more vicious revenge raids. These Apache raids were so numerous that in 1844, a Santa Fe trader observed that the "whole country from New Mexico to the borders of Durango is almost entirely depopulated" outside the established towns.

Yet at the same time, the Mexican state of Chihuahua, directly to the east of Sonora, became an Apache refuge. The Apache took the horses and mules they stole from Sonora and traded them for

26　GERONIMO

This picture depicts Geronimo and his band returning from a raid they took into Mexico. Although the Apache and the Mexicans had raided and traded with each other for centuries, their already uneasy relationship grew into warfare when Mexico placed a bounty on Apache scalps. The Apache retaliated with a series of deadly raids on Mexican villages.

cloth, knives, ammunition, and other articles in Chihuahua. In exchange for peaceful relations, Chihuahua even issued rations to the Apache. Sonora had no such policy. Both northern states were far from the center of Mexican power and population around Mexico City and often had to fend for themselves when it came to relations with Native Americans. In this case, the policies contradicted each other.

In the 1840s, Apache war parties had many fights with civilians and soldiers in Sonora. Geronimo took part in many of these, although the chronology of the raids is not certain. It appears that in January 1851 (again, the date from the Congressional Resolution is not correct), Geronimo and other Apache under Mangas Coloradas were returning north with 1,000 horses and cattle stolen in a particularly devastating raid. A Mexican force of 100 men under Captain Ignacio Pesqueira ambushed the Apache at Pozo Hediondo [Stinking Wells]. The Mexican troops surprised and routed the Apache's advance group. The Mexican soldiers excitedly chased the retreating warriors and ran straight into the main body of about 150 Chiricahua. The resulting clash, lasting several hours, was the most intense and bloody battle Geronimo had yet experienced.

The Mexicans suffered 72 killed and wounded. According to one version of the story, it was at this battle that the Mexicans gave Geronimo his now legendary name (Jerome in English). He repeatedly attacked Mexican soldiers with a knife, ignored a deadly hail of bullets, and so terrified the Mexicans that they called out to San Geronimo (Saint Jerome) for aid. The name stuck. Although this is a great story, it seems just as likely that he acquired the name through peaceful encounters with Mexicans, such as trading or negotiating.

TRAGEDY AT JANOS

The Apache victory at Pozo Hediondo had fateful consequences for Geronimo and his people. The commander of Sonora's small military force, Colonel José María Carrasco, determined to punish the

Apache in Chihuahua. He especially hated the Chiricahua who received rations at the town of Janos, Chihuahua. Carrasco suspected these Apache used Janos as a base to raid Sonora.

"I waited until the allotted time for the Apaches to visit Janos to obtain their regular quarterly rations," Carrasco later explained, and "by forced marches at night, succeeded in reaching the place just as the carnival was at its height." In March 1851, about 400 soldiers from Sonora attacked Geronimo's camp outside Janos while the warriors were in town trading and perhaps overdrinking. Carrasco's surprise attack was deadly. He killed at least 21 Apache and took 62 prisoners, mostly women and children.

Among those killed by the Mexicans were Geronimo's wife, Alope, his three children, and his mother, Juana. The remaining Apache, outnumbered and far from home, had to sneak back to their land in the north. For three days, Geronimo barely ate or said anything. He tried to talk "with the other Indians who had lost in the massacre, but none had lost as I had, for I had lost all."

When Geronimo arrived at his home village, he had to return to his lodge. Everything there reminded him of his wife and his dead children, from Alope's decorations in the wickiup to the children's toys strewn in the dirt. As was the Apache custom, he burned all of the property of his deceased family. He also burned his mother's teepee and destroyed all of her property.

Almost 50 years later, when Geronimo related this tragic chapter in his life to an acquaintance, the aged warrior became extremely upset. "He rose from his bed, his dark face almost white with anger as he shook his fist in my face, fairly hissing, as he declared, 'After that I killed every white man I saw.'"

The massacre at Janos completely unsettled Geronimo. "I was never again contented in our quiet home.... I had vowed vengeance upon the Mexican troopers who had wronged me, and whenever I ... saw anything to remind me of former happy days my heart would ache for revenge upon Mexico." In the next 30 years, Geronimo and his group of Chiricahua Apache would kill hundreds of Mexicans—soldiers and noncombatants alike. Yet his vengeance was never satisfied. Fifty-five years later, when Geronimo was in his eighties, he said, "It has been a long time since then, but still I have no love for the

Mexicans. With me, they were always treacherous and malicious. I am old now and shall never go on the warpath again, but if I were young, and followed the warpath, it would lead into Old Mexico."

Scalping and Torture

Scalping is the removal of all or part of the scalp, usually with hair attached, from an enemy's head. Scalps might be displayed as trophies or proofs of bravery. Americans who lived in Arizona in the 1800s believed that the Apache warriors scalped all their victims. Apache insist that scalping was infrequent and only used in bitter retaliation for American or Mexican atrocities. The truth was probably somewhere in between.

The Apache did practice scalping on occasion, especially for revenge, but it was never an important part of their ritual. A scalp might be taken for a victory dance, but the man who performed the act then had to participate in a four-day purification ceremony, during which time he remained in isolation. The Apache dreaded being scalped by their enemies. They believed mutilated victims would remain scarred and humiliated forever in The Happy Place.

Jason Betzinez said he never knew Geronimo to bring in a scalp. Another Apache who fought in these wars with Americans and Mexicans said, "I have seen hundreds of people killed but not one scalped." Victorio, the famous Apache chief, did not permit scalping under any circumstances.

On the other hand, Mexicans and Americans often practiced scalping, cut off other body parts, and killed children. By the 1800s, Mexicans, Americans, and Apache all committed atrocities on the bodies of their enemies. It is probably impossible to determine who learned scalping from whom. There was plenty of blame to go around.

However, scalping became associated with all Native Americans even though white Americans practiced it as much or more than Native tribes. It was a basic part of American propaganda to demonize the Native American. For example, the ridiculous story was circulated that when Geronimo surrendered, he was wearing a blanket made of 100 white scalps he had collected. The account even found its way into serious publications.

A LIFE OF CONSTANT RAIDING

Geronimo's own version of his life after the massacre of his family was the story of one bloody raid into Mexico after another. For 10 straight years, Geronimo raided Sonora and Chihuahua. Some were successful and some were failures; all were bloody. Geronimo was severely wounded and almost killed several times. Yet somehow, he survived. Although he was not a chief, his exploits in battle helped him rise to a position of leadership, especially in war, and made his reputation within the tribe. The decade of raiding into Mexico turned Geronimo into a master warrior and a leader of men.

Raids for the sake of vengeance were an honorable undertaking among the Apache. Revenge was not just a lawless rampage by an individual but a sacred social duty. A murder moved the state of the universe out of equilibrium; only revenge could balance the equation. Nor was it necessary to kill the particular person who had done the harm; anyone associated with the group that committed the original wrong would do.

Sometimes, Geronimo's raids into Mexico involved only two fellow warriors. Other times, the raiding party could number as many as 25. The Apache usually traveled on foot, for Geronimo noted, "we were accustomed to fight on foot; besides, we could more easily conceal ourselves when dismounted." If they wanted to steal cattle, however, they needed to travel by horse in order to drive the livestock.

Before departing on a large raid, warriors made careful preparations for the safety of the women, children, and elderly left behind. Usually, the camp would break apart and scatter in different directions. Then the people would reassemble at a predetermined location many miles away. "In this way, it would be hard for the Mexicans to trail them and we would know where to find our families when we returned," Geronimo said.

Apache raiders wore little more than moccasins and a cloth wrapped around their loins. The cloth doubled as a blanket and could be spread over the warrior when he slept. "In battle, if the fight was hard, we did not wish much clothing," Geronimo noted. Each

As a war leader, Geronimo was believed to have special abilities known as Power. Apache men willingly followed him into battle through Mexican villages, and later against American settlers in the Southwest, even when outnumbered. Here, Geronimo (*right*) is pictured with some Apache warriors.

warrior carried enough rations for about three days but they added to this by killing game along the way. Raiders might march about 14 hours a day, making three stops for meals. In this way, they could travel about 40 miles (64 km) a day.

Geronimo led many of these raids. He still thirsted for revenge against the Mexicans who killed his family. Other Apache were not driven by the same motivation. Even Geronimo admitted he sometimes had to work hard to convince other warriors to go with him.

The raids almost seemed like a children's game, except that they usually resulted in tragedy for both sides. The Apache killed Mexicans without remorse, and the Mexicans felt the same way. No mercy was asked, and none was expected. The Apache wanted no witnesses to their movements; "if we passed a Mexican's home we usually killed the inmates," Geronimo said. In Apachería, violence could affect a person's life at any time. "Until I was about ten years old," said one Apache warrior, "I did not know that people died except by violence."

FAMILY LIFE

It is almost impossible to sort out Geronimo's complicated family life. Polygamy was an accepted practice of Chiricahua life. Apache peoples, like most preindustrial cultures, divided economic activities between men and women. A person whose spouse died usually remarried quickly by necessity. The Apache were always extremely family oriented. Blood relationship formed exceptionally strong bonds involving mutual aid and responsibilities that could not be broken easily.

Geronimo's wives came and went, overlapping each other, being captured and added to the family, lost, killed, or even given up. Geronimo once said that "he might have had as many wives as he wished, but he ... was so busy fighting Mexicans that he could not support more than two." Nonetheless, there were times when Geronimo seems to have had as many as three wives. In general, he seems to have loved his wives and they loved him, and worked well with one another.

Sometime in the 1850s, Geronimo married Cheehashkish, also a Bedonkohe. They would have a son (Chappo) and a daughter (Dohnsay). Shortly afterward, Geronimo married another Bedonkohe woman, Nanathathtith. She had one child by Geronimo whose name was not recorded. Geronimo's feelings toward Mexicans could not have been improved when an attack by Mexican troops left Nanathathtith and their child dead.

"I Had Lost All" 33

Geronimo had several wives over his lifetime, sometimes overlapping each other. This is a studio portrait of Marlanetta (also called Marionetta or Early Morning), who may have been the seventh or possibly eighth wife of Geronimo.

In the early 1860s, Geronimo married Shesha, a Nednhi, and then a Bedonkohe woman named Shtshashe. Some of his wives were captured, such as the young Ihtedda, when his band surrendered. Geronimo also had several wives in captivity; his last wife was Azul.

It is hard to tell for sure, but Geronimo seems to have had nine wives and about eleven children, though less than half of them survived to adulthood. This was not unusual for a prominent Chiricahua. However, no woman seems to have ever been as close to his heart as his first wife, the murdered Alope.

GERONIMO'S POWER

The Chiricahua Apache thought that supernatural Power filled the universe. This Power could be used to do things such as cure illnesses, defeat an enemy, and find lost objects. A person might use Power to protect himself (or herself) and his family, or it might be used in rites to help the entire tribe.

Power also had evil aspects. The Apache believed in witches. These were men and women whose evil Power brought misfortune to individuals or the group. Power was the life force of the universe and sought out individuals through which to work.

Unlike many other Native tribes, the Apache did not believe that only shamans or medicine men possessed all the Power. Instead, they thought almost any man or woman could have one kind of Power or another. Humans could reach Power through plants, animals, and other natural phenomena that would take human form to teach an Apache man or woman the correct ceremonies.

It was also unusual for an Apache to go off alone on a conscious spiritual quest or vision experience. Power came to a person suddenly and unexpectedly; its nature and the way it came varied from person to person. The experience tested the courage and determination of the individual.

Geronimo received his first gift of Power after the murder of his family at Janos. Geronimo's Power told him that, "No gun can ever kill you." Geronimo followed this Power wherever it led him, even through the bullets of his enemies. The fact that he was often wounded (at least eight times) strengthened his belief. When he was an old man, he bared himself to the waist to show a white acquaintance the number of bullet holes in his body. He said simply, "Bullets cannot kill me." Geronimo later acquired other attributes of Power. He supposedly could tell what was happening in distant places, make predictions about the future, and sometimes heal the sick.

The Apache considered Geronimo a medicine man (or shaman) and his Power was expressed through special songs and prayers. He often consulted his Power to make military decisions. Fifty years later, one of Geronimo's followers remembered that he would go through his ceremony and announce, "'You should go here; you should not go there.' That is how he became a leader." His nephew said that Geronimo's warriors "were with him in many dangerous times and saw his miraculous escapes, his cures for wounds, and the results of his medicine; so his warriors knew that Geronimo was alive only because of Ussen's protection."

4

ENTER THE AMERICANS

In 1848, a new player entered the bloody world of Apache-Mexican relations. In that year, the United States defeated Mexico and took one-third of Mexico's territory, including the present-day states of California, New Mexico, and Arizona. The early relations between the Apache and the Americans were friendly. The Apache looked kindly upon anyone fighting and killing Mexicans. They allowed American armies during the war to pass through their territories unmolested.

The Apache were less pleased with the peace, however. The Treaty of Guadalupe Hidalgo contained a pledge that the American government would keep the Apache in its newly acquired territory from raiding Mexico. The U.S. government also promised to return any captives that the Apache captured on these raids into Mexico. These promises caused immediate tension between the Apache and the Americans.

When the California Gold Rush began in 1849, thousands of prospectors headed west to the gold fields. Some traveled through Apachería, while others drifted south after failing to strike it rich in northern California. The flood of whites strained U.S.-Apache relations. One Apache told a U.S. Army quartermaster, "We must steal

U.S. Annexation of Mexican Land, 1845–1853

Map legend:
- Ceded by Mexico, 1848
- Annexed by U.S., 1845
- Gadsden Purchase, 1853
- Fort

Map labels include: Canada; Oregon Territory; Minnesota Territory; Wisconsin; Unorganized Territory; United States; Iowa; Missouri; Arkansas; Louisiana; Mexico. Cities/forts: Salt Lake City, Denver, Bent's Fort, San Francisco, Las Vegas, Santa Fe, Albuquerque, Los Angeles, Tucson, El Paso, Chihuahua, San Antonio, Monterrey, Fort Smith. Rivers: Columbia R., Snake R., Sacramento R., Colorado R., Gila R., Missouri R., Platte R., Arkansas R., Red R., Rio Grande, Mississippi R.

Annotations on map:
- Purchased from Texas by U.S., 1850
- Disputed by Mexico and Texas from 1836
- Assigned to Texas by U.S., 1850
- Texas: Independent of Mexico, 1835; Republic, 1836; Admitted as state, 1845

© Infobase Publishing

With the Treaty of Guadalupe Hidalgo (1848), Mexico ceded most of its northern region to the United States for $15 million, and the treaty extended U.S. citizenship to Mexicans in those territories, years before African Americans, Asians, and Native Americans were eligible. Five years later, the Gadsden Purchase rounded out America's permanent continental boundaries with the purchase of another 29,000 square miles of territory in southern Arizona and New Mexico.

from somebody; and if you will not permit us to rob the Mexicans, we must steal from you or fight you."

Then, in 1854, the United States bought additional land from Mexico. In this so-called Gadsden Purchase, the United States paid $10 million for a small strip of land (about 29,000 square miles or

The Butterfield Overland Mail

After California became a state in 1850, the federal government had to find some way to get the mail there in a timely manner. In 1858, the government agreed to pay John Butterfield $600,000 per year for carrying the mail. Butterfield invested $1 million into setting up the route, using more than 200 coaches and almost 2,000 horses and mules. Among the 1,200 employees were superintendents, drivers, conductors, harness makers, and blacksmiths. Butterfield sent workers out along the route to build 200 stations and relay posts, and to make sure the roads were passable between them.

The Overland Mail route began at Memphis, Tennessee, and St. Louis, Missouri, joined at Fort Smith, Arkansas, then went south to El Paso, Texas, across southern New Mexico and Arizona to Fort Yuma, and up California's central valley to San Francisco. This "Oxbow Route" was about 2,800 miles (4,506 km), an extra 600 miles (970 km) longer than the central and northern routes running through Denver, Colorado, and Salt Lake City, Utah. However, the southern route had the advantage of being snow-free year-round. In its history, the Overland Mail was attacked only once by Apache. The Butterfield line ended in March 1861 just before the beginning of the Civil War.

It took 24 days for the mail to travel from St. Louis to San Francisco. Stages traveled about 120 miles (193 km) each day. Passengers received two daily breaks and 40 minutes rest while eating at a way station. One passenger wrote, "The fatigue of uninterrupted traveling by day and night in a crowded coach, and in the most uncomfortable positions, was . . . producing in me a condition bordering on insanity."

Waterman Ormsby was a *New York Herald* reporter who rode the entire way on the first westbound trip. He wrote that he found the Butterfield employees, "without exception, to be courteous, civil, and attentive." He concluded, however, "Had I not just come out over the route, I would be perfectly willing to go back, but I now know what Hell is like. I've just had 24 days of it."

75,000 sq km) across southern Arizona and New Mexico south of the Gila River. This purchase included the heart of Chiricahua Apache territory. The United States wanted the land for use as a right of way for a southern transcontinental railroad to the Pacific coast.

In 1856, the U.S. Army began a long presence in southern Arizona when they established Fort Buchanan, 25 miles (40 km) east of the Hispanic settlement of Tubac. The fort's mission was to guard the few Anglo ranchers and miners of the region against Apache threats. The Apache were not pleased with this military intrusion in their land. "From the very first," Geronimo said, "the soldiers sent out to our western country, and the officers in charge of them, did not hesitate to wrong the Indians."

A southern transcontinental railroad would not be built for many years. However, in 1858, the Butterfield Overland Mail began carrying letters on a long southern route between St. Louis and San Francisco. One of the stage line's many relay stations was located in Apache Pass, a natural route between the Dos Cabezas Mountains in the north and the Chiricahua Mountains in the south, and the site of an important spring.

"THE CUT THROUGH THE TENT" AFFAIR

For several years, the Chiricahua Apache maintained wary relations with the Americans and the employees of the Butterfield Overland Mail. Tensions rose as Apache raiding on both sides of the border continued, and contact and conflicts with ranchers and miners became more frequent.

Cochise was the powerful chief of the Chokonen band of the Chiricahua. He was the son-in-law of Mangas Coloradas, the respected leader of all the Apache of southwestern New Mexico. Cochise had tolerated the employees and drivers of the Butterfield Mail line and had no particular reason to attack Americans.

This changed after an incident in 1861 at the Apache Pass stage station. U.S. Lieutenant George Bascom wanted to gain the release of a boy supposedly seized in an Apache raid near Fort Buchanan. He summoned Cochise to a meeting at Apache Pass. Then Bascom made a terrible blunder by attempting to capture Cochise and hold him for ransom. In fact, Cochise's people were not the culprits. Bascom also underestimated the determination and courage of Cochise, who escaped by slashing the officer's tent with his knife and making a wild dash for safety.

Some of Cochise's relatives who had accompanied him to Apache Pass could not escape with their chief, so Bascom held them as hostages instead. Cochise immediately began gathering his own hostages, attacking anyone unfortunate enough to be traveling in the area. In the end, several days passed and there was no agreement or exchange. Cochise executed his prisoners, and the Americans hung six Apache warriors.

This tragic "Cut Through the Tent Affair" (known to Americans as the "Bascom Affair") led to a bloody war between the Chiricahua Apache and the Americans. "There was no general engagement," Geronimo remembered, "but a long struggle followed. Sometimes we attacked the white men—sometimes they attacked us.... I think the killing was about equal on each side. The number killed in these troubles did not amount to much, but the treachery on the part of the soldiers had angered the Indians and revived memories of other wrongs, so that we never again trusted the United States troops."

After his relatives were executed, Cochise hated the Americans as much as Geronimo hated the Mexicans. Cochise did not care that only a few Americans had wronged him; he hated them all. Cochise began to apply the Apache punishment for witches—hanging men head-down from trees and roasting them over a slow fire—to American captives. Americans responded in kind. The Bascom Affair ignited a bloody cycle of revenge and retaliation that would last 10 years. Geronimo was probably involved in many of the battles; he said, "I had not been wronged, but some of my people had been, and I fought with my tribe."

Geronimo was probably not present in the "Cut Through the Tent Affair." He did take part in an ambush of a group of California Volunteers marching eastward through Apache Pass on July

Built in 1862 after a series of violent conflicts between the U.S. Army and the Chiricahua, Fort Bowie served as the U.S. Army's headquarters in its campaign to defeat Cochise and Geronimo. In this picture, cavalry are riding away from Fort Bowie on patrol.

15, 1862. About 100 Apache warriors led by Cochise and Mangas Coloradas opened fire on the soldiers from the protected heights overlooking the abandoned stage station.

The California Volunteers had a surprise weapon. They wheeled two howitzers to use against the entrenched Apache. This would be one of the only times that the U.S. Army used artillery successfully against Native Americans. The Chiricahua reluctantly abandoned the important spring to the soldiers. This "Battle of Apache Pass" resulted in the establishment of Fort Bowie near the spring. The fort would become the headquarters of the campaigns against Geronimo and the Chiricahua Apache. Almost a century later, the son of a chief who fought there said, "After they turned cannon loose on us at Apache Pass, my people were certain that they were doomed."

"PERHAPS THE GREATEST WRONG EVER DONE TO THE INDIANS"

The U.S. Civil War began in 1861 and Union and Confederate forces fought for ownership of Arizona. However, both the Blue and the Gray supported a war of extermination against the Apache occupants of the land. Colonel John Baylor, the Confederate military governor of Arizona, ordered his men in Tucson to buy whiskey and "persuade the Apaches or any tribe to come in for the purpose of making peace, and when you get them together, kill all the grown Indians and take the children prisoners and sell them to defray the expense of killing the Indians." The Union Army was no friendlier. In 1862, Union general James Carlton told his soldiers, "All Indian men of that tribe [the Mescalero Apache] are to be killed whenever and wherever you can find them."

These types of attitudes could only lead to trouble. Yet, in January 1863, Mangas Coloradas had decided that the only solution for the Apache tribes was to make peace with the Americans. This most-respected of Apache chiefs took half his people to the mining settlement of Pinos Altos, New Mexico Territory. The Americans there had assured him that the Apache could live near them in peace and receive government rations.

Instead, the Americans led the trusting chief into a trap. He was taken prisoner and turned over to the U.S. Army at Fort McLane. He was probably tortured while in captivity and in the early morning of January 19, 1863, Mangas was murdered by his guards while supposedly attempting to escape. Then, someone severed the great chief's head from his body. His brain was taken out and weighed, and his head was boiled to obtain his skull. According to legend, the skull was sent to Washington, D.C., and supposedly exhibited at the Smithsonian Museum.

The Apache were horrified. They believed that a person traveled in the Happy Place in the physical state in which they died. The Chiricahua pictured their great chief wandering headless through eternity. Geronimo would later say that this grisly incident was "perhaps the greatest wrong ever done to the Indians."

In the 1970s, researchers who studied the Chiricahua living in New Mexico and Oklahoma discovered that more of them knew the "Cut Through the Tent Affair" and the murder of Mangas Coloradas than remembered the Japanese attack on Pearl Harbor in 1941. Most Apache insist that it was only in response to the mutilation of Mangas' body that they began to regularly butcher white corpses.

THE APACHE WARS

Geronimo, unlike Mangas Coloradas, did not trust the Americans. Mangas' murder and subsequent attacks on the Chiricahua put Geronimo's group in a bad situation because they had given Mangas most of their arms and ammunition. They were forced to flee deeper into the mountains. The Bedonkohe band, weakened in numbers, broke apart and never reassembled. The surviving Bedonkohe joined the other three Chiricahua bands: the Chokonen under Cochise, the Chihenne under Victorio, and the Nednhi under Juh (spelled many different ways but pronounced "Ho").

Juh was a childhood friend of Geronimo's. He had married a cousin of Geronimo's so it was natural that Geronimo join Juh's band. "Their Chief, Whoa [Juh], was as a brother to me," Geronimo recalled, "and we spent much of our time in his territory." For the next few years, almost nothing is known of Geronimo's activities. Juh and his band probably spent most of their time attacking Mexicans and hiding in the almost inaccessible mountains of northern Chihuahua and Sonora. In 1871, Geronimo was almost certainly with Juh's band when they ambushed and killed the noted "Indian fighter" U.S. lieutenant Howard Cushing.

At the same time, Cochise's warriors spent the 1860s rampaging across Arizona, killing any prospectors, ranchers, stagecoach passengers, farmers, and soldiers he happened to find. Because of the Civil War, the United States abandoned the forts in the Arizona Territory and shifted the soldiers to the east. By late 1861, only two pockets of white settlement remained in Arizona: a small mining camp at Patagonia and the lawless town of Tucson with about 200 inhabitants.

In the 10 years after the "Cut Through the Tent Affair," the U.S. government spent an estimated $38 million on military campaigns that killed about 100 Apache. The Apache, meanwhile, may have killed as many as 1,000 Americans. The U.S. Board of Indian Commissioners reported to President Ulysses Grant in December 1871 that since 1861, the U.S. Army had attempted to exterminate the Apache "at a cost of from three to four million dollars per annum, with no appreciable progress being made in accomplishing the extermination." Even white Americans grudgingly admitted Cochise's courage and military skill.

When the Civil War ended in 1865, and the transcontinental railroad was completed in 1869, prospectors, miners, ranchers, and adventurers moved in increasing numbers to New Mexico and Arizona (the two territories were separated in 1863). The U.S. census for 1860 listed only 2,421 citizens; by 1870, the number was 9,658, including about half of Mexican origin and about 2,100 troops. At the same time, about 7,000 Apache lived in the Southwest of which between 1,000 and 2,000 were Chiricahua.

THE CAMP GRANT MASSACRE

The Apache generally preferred to deal with the U.S. Army. They knew they could expect no justice or mercy from the citizens of Arizona. This became perfectly clear after the Camp Grant Massacre in Arizona in 1871.

The Aravaipa, under their famous war chief Eskiminzin, had been hunted and harassed to the brink of starvation. A generous U.S. Army officer, Royal Whitman, allowed the band to camp near the post at Camp Grant and tried to get them a reservation.

As they waited, Tucson settlers blamed Eskininzin's band for several raids and murders near Tucson. At dawn of April 30, vigilantes from Tucson attacked the Aravaipa while their warriors were away hunting. Six of the attackers were white Americans, 48 were Mexicans, and 92 were Papago Indians, traditional enemies of the Apache. Most of the Aravaipa were hacked and clubbed to death while they slept. Royal Whitman testified that his troops found and buried 125 bodies. Only eight of them were men, the rest were women and children. According to the army surgeon from Camp Grant, nearly all the dead bodies were mutilated, including infants.

Newspapers in San Francisco and Denver applauded the murderers and congratulated them on their "permanent peace arrangements." The publisher of the *Arizona Citizen* praised the attack and called the Apache peoples "untamable brutes; fit for nothing but slaughter." William Oury, one of the raiding party's leaders, took credit for the "killing of 144 of the most blood-thirsty Devils that ever disgraced mother Earth." Oury Park in Tucson today honors the pioneer who organized the massacre.

King Woolsey

The Apache could be brutal, but for sheer treachery, they were no match for white Americans. In territorial Arizona, a sleazy cold-blooded murderer like King Woolsey (c. 1832–1879) was considered a great hero.

In 1864, after a series of livestock thefts, Woolsey led a group of settlers to attack any Apache they found. Near present-day Miami, Arizona, they encountered a large party of Tonto Apache. Woolsey pretended he wanted to talk peace and lured the Natives into a parley [conference]. Then he and his men opened fire and murdered 24 Apache in cold blood.

Later that year, Woolsey and several other men were working their mining claims when they met a large party of Yavapai. Woolsey called for a parley, after first hiding a sack of corn meal poisoned with strychnine nearby. As Woolsey hoped, the Yavapai found the poisoned meal and ate it while he talked to their chiefs. As the poison took effect, and the others fled, Woolsey's men opened fire on them. Because of this brave action, the Arizona Territorial Legislature voted to commend King Woolsey and his volunteers for "taking the lives of numbers of Apaches, and destroying the property and crops in their country." Woolsey later served in several Arizona legislatures.

However, the massacre generated national sympathy for the Apache. President Ulysses Grant told Governor Anson Safford that if the perpetrators were not brought to trial, he would place Arizona under martial law. In October 1871, a Tucson grand jury indicted 100 of the assailants with 108 counts of murder. The trial lasted five days and focused only on Apache raids. The federal government did not call any Apache as witnesses. After only 19 minutes of deliberation, the jury acquitted every defendant. Arizonans simply would not convict a man for killing an Apache, even if that Apache was a child. "Nits make lice," they said. Many Arizona settlers believed that only extermination would solve the Apache problem.

THE FORT BOWIE RESERVATION

The U.S. Army finally conceded that it was more cost effective to pursue a peace policy. Cochise's friendship with Thomas Jeffords, a white American, became the key to peace. In 1872, General Oliver Otis Howard, the U.S. Indian commissioner, requested that Jeffords arrange a meeting with Cochise in his Dragoon Mountain stronghold in southeastern Arizona. In the end, Cochise agreed to live on the reservation that Howard promised would be created from the chief's native territory.

The president signed the order creating the 3,000-square-mile (7,769-sq-km) Fort Bowie Reservation in southeastern Arizona on December 14, 1872. The Apache would settle near an army camp and agree not to raid or steal. In return, the U.S. government would give the Apache rations, clothing, and protection from lawless white settlers.

It is not clear if Geronimo took part in this famous meeting between Cochise and O.O. Howard. However, Geronimo and Juh did bring their people to the Fort Bowie Reservation. For the rest of his life, Geronimo would remember Howard with affection and gratitude. Geronimo said, "This treaty lasted until long after General Howard had left our country. He always kept his word with us and treated us as brothers."

General O.O. Howard was sent by President Ulysses Grant to Arizona as a peace commissioner with instructions to establish a reservation for the Apache. By 1872, five agencies had been designated, and most of the bands agreed to resettle in exchange for food and supplies. Still, some Apache, including Geronimo, continued to resist settlement.

The Apache were satisfied with the reservation. It was 55 miles (88 km) wide, adjoined Sonora—sharing an extensive border with Arizona, and was independent from the U.S. Army. The reservation included Cochise's Dragoon Mountain stronghold, Apache Pass with its important spring, and dozens of canyons full of antelope and deer. "Rations were issued about once a month," recalled Geronimo, "but if we ran out, we only had to ask and we were supplied." If rations were slow in coming, the Chiricahua could live by raiding into Mexico and by hunting and gathering as they had for centuries. A single trustworthy Indian agent—Tom Jeffords—supervised more than 1,000 Chiricahua.

Cochise only lived two more years, but for that time, he kept most of the Chiricahua at peace with the Americans in southeastern Arizona. However, he did very little to prevent continued Apache raiding across the Mexican border into Sonora.

GENERAL GEORGE CROOK

George Crook was the greatest "Indian fighter" ever produced by the U.S. Army. After attending West Point, Crook spent the 1850s battling Native tribes in northern California and southern Oregon. During the Civil War, Crook was present at the bloody battles of Antietam, Chickamauga, Chattanooga, and Shenandoah Valley, and was there at Robert E. Lee's final surrender at Appomattox Court House. Throughout the war, he performed well, sometimes brilliantly, and always courageously under fire. The hard-fighting Crook earned Ulysses Grant's respect.

Crook was an unusual general in many ways. He often chose to ride a mule rather than a horse. He rarely wore his uniform in the field and had a reputation as a modest man who looked more like an improperly dressed volunteer than a commanding general. Throughout his life, he was calm, aloof, and self-confident; some called him gloomy. Crook did not drink alcohol, coffee, or tea; his great passion was hunting, which he pursued at every opportunity. He knew how to pack a mule, mend a saddle, throw a lariat (lasso), and cook a meal in the field. As a commander, he was easy to respect but perhaps hard to like.

Crook first came to the Southwest in 1871. He soon developed the only tactics that succeeded in defeating the Apache. He decided that Civil War tactics would not work against warriors who would not stand and fight. Instead, Crook drilled his soldiers on rapid pursuit. He discarded the clumsy army supply wagons and developed the use of mule pack trains. "He made the study of pack-trains the great study of his life," his chief aide said. Crook's mules, with their custom-fitted packsaddles, could carry 320 pounds (145 kilograms) compared to the army standard of 175 pounds (79 kg).

He also enlisted Apache scouts, "the wilder the better" he said, for trailing Apache and then for much of the fighting. His experience on the frontier convinced him that he needed gifted trackers with a deep knowledge of the country. He supposedly said, "It takes an Apache to catch an Apache."

In the winter of 1872–1873, Crook began a brutal campaign against the tribes of western Arizona who refused to come to the reservations. He was successful, and by spring, most surviving raiders began to settle on the reservations. Crook was rewarded with a startling promotion from lieutenant colonel to brigadier general.

After the Native Americans surrendered, Crook generally tried to treat them fairly. He tried to avoid lying to the tribes and refused to promise anything he could not deliver. The Apache viewed Crook as a relentless but honest enemy. It was a rare concession, for the Apache had learned through their experiences that most whites were habitual liars.

At the same time, Crook viewed Native Americans with a combination of racist scorn and sympathy. He believed they were doomed to extinction or assimilation and worked all his life to destroy their cultures, hunt down their warriors, and seize their land.

Yet he had nothing but contempt for the U.S. Army and the U.S. government that he felt disregarded his wisdom and disrespected his accomplishments. "I do not wonder ... that when these Indians see their wives and children starving, and their last source of supplies cut off, they go to war," Crook said. "And then we are sent out to kill them. It is an outrage."

In 1874, Cochise died of stomach cancer. Tom Jeffords tried to maintain order, but some young Apache grew discontented with the reservation and escaped. However, the situation was probably salvageable and the Apache wars seemed to be in process of settlement. In 1875, Apache-American relations were in the most hopeful state since the wars began. Arizona's Governor Safford told the legislature, "Comparative peace now reigns throughout the Territory, with almost a certainty that no general Indian war will ever occur again."

Then, the U.S. Indian Department intervened and threw the Southwest into turmoil for a decade.

5

SAN CARLOS

In 1875, the U.S. Department of the Interior made a massive mistake that led to the deaths of hundreds of civilians in the United States and Mexico and the near-extinction of the Apache. The bureaucrats in Washington, D.C., ordered all the Apache west of the Rio Grande to the arid San Carlos Reservation in southeastern Arizona. The U.S. government wanted to concentrate all the Apache tribes together on one reservation. This cruel uprooting of the barely settled Apache, who had only recently been guaranteed a homeland forever, resulted in 11 more years of Apache wars.

In October 1876, President Grant officially revoked the Chiricahua Reservation that Cochise had won four years earlier and returned the land to the public domain. This policy meant Geronimo's tribe would have to leave their beloved Chiricahua Mountains. Taza, Cochise's eldest son and successor, and 325 Chiricahua were moved to the parched San Carlos Reservation. Crook, now a brigadier general, strongly opposed the measure, but in March 1875 he was transferred to the northern plains to fight the Sioux and their Cheyenne and Arapaho allies. His successors, General August Kautz and then general Orlando Wilcox, were left to deal with the inevitable hostilities.

Geronimo refused to move to the hot, barren, and disease-ridden Gila River Valley. Instead, he and Juh led several bands—more than 100 warriors—to the Sierra Madre of northern Mexico.

As Juh noted, "Hadn't they always been a free people, roaming where they wished and living as Ussen had promised they should, free and in their own land?" However, living away from the reservation meant no more government rations. In order to survive, the Apache split into smaller bands and began to terrorize the border region. They were soon known by white people as "renegades" or "hostiles."

After raiding and battling soldiers all winter, Geronimo appeared at the Ojo Caliente (Warm Springs) Reservation with about 100 followers and another 100 stolen horses. This reservation was the home of Victorio's Chihenne band, often called the Warm Springs Apache. Geronimo used the reservation as a base to make raids in Arizona and Mexico. Then he would return to the government agency in the hopes of receiving blankets and rations.

CAPTURED

Orders now came from Washington, D.C., to arrest Geronimo and remove him to San Carlos. That difficult job fell to 26-year-old Indian agent John Clum. On April 21, 1877, Clum hid his Indian police (including Naiche, Geronimo's youngest son) in the Ojo Caliente commissary building. Then he requested a conference with Geronimo.

The unsuspecting warrior entered Clum's trap. When Clum informed Geronimo of his orders, Geronimo defiantly told him, "We are not going to San Carlos with you, and unless you are very careful, you and your Apache police will not go back to San Carlos, either. Your bodies will stay here at Ojo Caliente to make food for the coyotes." Clum marched out his hidden reserves and disarmed the Chiricahua leader and his men. To the end of his long life, Clum remembered that when he took Geronimo's rifle, "I have seen many looks of hate in my long life, but never one so vicious, so vengeful . . . " This was the only time in his life that Geronimo was actually captured and it had taken a trick to do it. As he later noted to the U.S. Army, "you never have caught me shooting."

Clum put Geronimo and six other "renegade" Apache in chains and marched them to San Carlos. Amazingly, without any explanation, the Americans also removed Victorio's Chihenne people to San Carlos. The removal of the Warm Springs band was particularly unwise, and it would have tragic and bloody consequences. As late as the 1950s, members of the tribe still insisted that, "We were innocent and should not have been driven from our homes. We were not to blame for what Geronimo did. The United States didn't give this land to us. It was ours." However, like the Apache, the U.S. government did not usually differentiate the individual from the group; an Apache was an Apache.

Clum's orders stated that Geronimo and the other "renegades" should be tried at San Carlos for murder and robbery. The agent prepared to turn Geronimo and the other prisoners over to the sheriff in Tucson for trial and inevitable hanging. Fortunately for Geronimo, the arrogant Clum became involved in a huge power struggle with the U.S. Army over who had authority at San Carlos. Clum angrily resigned his position in July 1877. His successor, Henry Lyman Hart, ordered Geronimo released from the guardhouse.

Years later, Clum told his friends that he "should have hung Geronimo over at Hot Springs and never bothered about bringing him to San Carlos." Clum would later be mayor of Tombstone, Arizona, in its bloody heyday. All his life, he would blame Geronimo for almost every single problem with the Apache in Arizona.

LIFE AT SAN CARLOS

"San Carlos! That was the worst place in all the great territory stolen from the Apaches," remembered one member of the tribe. "Where there is no grass, there is no game. Nearly all of the vegetation was cacti.... The water was terrible. What there was in the sluggish river was brackish and warm.... Insects and rattlesnakes seemed to thrive there...." A U.S. Army officer called it "Hell's Forty Acres." He described it as "almost continuously dry, hot, dust- and gravel-laden winds swept the plain, denuding it of every vestige of vegetation. In summer a temperature of 110° [Fahrenheit, 43° Celsius] in the shade was cool weather...." The government chose the location because it was relatively close to Tucson,

In 1875, U.S. officials ordered all Apache west of the Rio Grande to report to the San Carlos Reservation on the Gila River in Arizona (*above*). San Carlos was established in one of the lowest and hottest parts of the territory, and away from the vast forests and sacred mountains of the Chiricahua's homeland.

where the powerful merchants lived, and because the open terrain made it easier for the army to operate if necessary. Whether the Apache would like San Carlos was not a consideration.

In 1877, more than a thousand Chiricahua Apache lived at San Carlos, sharing the reservation with another 3,000 Western Apache, Yavapai, and Mojave. The Chiricahua were resentful and suspicious, and most of the bands were homesick. Bickering and then fighting broke out between the different groups. Smallpox and malaria began to spread. There were not many ways to make a living at San Carlos. Some of the Apache sold wild hay and firewood to the soldiers stationed there. Most lived on government rations of beef, flour, and corn to make it through the winter.

For a while, Geronimo and Juh led a quiet life on the reservation. Geronimo recalled, "We were allowed to live above San Carlos at a place now called Geronimo.... All went well for a period of two years, but we were not satisfied." Although Geronimo promised that he would not flee, he broke that pledge on August 2, 1878. The exact reasons for his flight are not clear. It may have been that his nephew committed suicide after Geronimo scolded him during a drinking spree. The Indian agent reported that Geronimo fled because the incident would reveal that his band was making illegal tizwin and Geronimo "was afraid of being put in the guardhouse."

From a hideout in the Sierra Madres, Geronimo and Juh resumed their raids into Sonora, stealing supplies and killing Mexicans. After a year of this, Juh and Geronimo sent peace overtures to the military in the fall of 1879 and returned to reservation life at San Carlos in the winter.

San Carlos had not gotten any better. After Clum's departure, a succession of weak or corrupt Indian agents helped destroy Apache morale and ruin any possibility of a peaceful settlement. Joseph Tiffany, according to one Apache, "was the worst agent San Carlos ever had." A grand jury reviewed his performance and called it "a disgrace to the civilization of the age.... As honest American citizens [we] express our abhorrence of the conduct of Agent Tiffany and that class of reverend peculators who have cursed Arizona as Indian officials, and who have caused more misery and loss of life than all other causes combined." When 11 Apaches had the courage to question the wagonloads of supplies that left the reservation, Tiffany imprisoned them without charges for more than a year. The grand jury noted, "With the immense power wielded by the Indian agent almost any crime is possible. There seems to be no check upon his conduct."

THE TUCSON RING

The Arizona and New Mexico territories were remote and isolated boundary areas. In 1874, it was 700 miles (1,126 km) from San Carlos to the nearest railroad depot. A military telegraph line—a single wire—ran from San Diego to Santa Fe. There was very little stage transportation and, of course, no telephone. Mail reached San Carlos once a week only if a messenger traveled 80 miles (128 km) to the nearest post office to get it. There were few ranches, ranges, or even mines. In this environment, supplying the army with food, forage, horses, and equipment was one of the leading industries in the territory. In this way, the U.S. government spread several million dollars a year through the economy of the Southwest.

The "Tucson Ring" was the name given to a group of corrupt army contractors and Tucson merchants. The Tucson Ring did not want peace in Arizona because that would lead to an economic crisis. One Tucson merchant complained to John Clum that peace would "ruin my business. If you take the military contracts away from us, there would be nothing worth staying for. Most of our profit comes from feeding soldiers and army mules." General Edward Ord stated that war was the foundation of the Arizona economy and that civilians demanded more troops because they wanted profit, not peace.

The Tucson Ring also schemed with Indian agents like Joseph Tiffany to furnish substandard rations to Indian reservations at regular prices. Then, the men would split the profits. Sometimes, with the aid of a reservation agent, they furnished no rations at all and pocketed all the money. One U.S. Army officer said, "The 'Tucson Ring' was determined that no Apache should be put to the embarrassment of working for his own living; once let the Apaches become self-supporting and what would become of 'the boys'?"

Many army officers believed that the Tucson Ring even operated secretly to actively promote incidents and American Indian scares. There is some evidence that several Anglo- and Mexican-Americans were involved in murderous "Indian style" raids on isolated settlements of whites in early 1871. The merchants wanted the lucrative contracts supplying grain, hay, and provisions for the soldiers sent to quell uprisings. Sometimes, "the boys" would simply generate an American Indian scare through their newspapers, claiming the Apache were uneasy. Then they would bombard Washington with requests for protection.

There is some question whether the Tucson Ring actually existed as an organized conspiracy rather than just a collection of immoral and greedy merchants. However, George Crook believed the Tucson Ring was real and blamed them for many of his difficulties. "When the Indian appeals to arms, his only redress, the whole country cries out against the Indian," Crook said. "As soon as the Indians became settled on the different reservations, gave up the warpath, and became harmless, the Indian agents . . . took charge of the agencies and commenced their game of plundering. . . . The American Indian commands respect for his rights only so long as he inspires terror with his rifle."

VICTORIO

Victorio was the chief of the Warm Springs band of the Chiricahua Apache. Between 1870 and 1877, Victorio did little raiding. His people were perfectly satisfied to live on their ancestral territory on the Ojo Caliente reservation by the Alamosa River. "That is a good country," remembered a Chihenne, 30 years later. "There are mountains on this side and on that side, and on the other side. In the middle, there is a wide valley. There are springs in that valley, fine grass, and plenty of timber around. . . . Horses and cattle will not freeze there. It is a healthy place for man and beast. Women nor children get sick there." When allowed to remain in that area, Victorio observed the peace. Any attempt to relocate him brought war.

58 GERONIMO

In April 1877, just when Apache crops were beginning to ripen, the U.S. government foolishly ordered Victorio and his band to move to the desolate reservation at San Carlos. In September, about

Despite his request to live on ancestral lands, Chief Victorio and his people were moved to several reservations. Victorio escaped the harsh conditions of San Carlos and led several hundred Apache on raids on white settlers around New Mexico. In 1880, he and his band were captured and killed by Mexican soldiers at Tres Castillos in northern Mexico.

300 of the Warm Springs band broke away. After some brutal raiding, they made their way to their old reservation at Ojo Caliente. There was no reason why they should not have been allowed to stay. However, the U.S. government felt otherwise. In October 1878, orders arrived from Washington to move the Warm Springs Apache to San Carlos again. Victorio pleaded with the army to allow his people to keep the land that had been theirs but the government was not responsive. Victorio refused to go and fled with many of his warriors.

Victorio established a stronghold in Mexico and began recruiting a guerrilla army "to make war forever" against the United States. At its peak, Victorio's band numbered about 450 Apache of which about 100 were warriors. The band terrorized the border country with repeated raids and massacres. For more than a year, his raiders eluded their pursuers, including the famous African-American "Buffalo Soldiers."

Victorio was a brilliant strategist using surprise attack, ambush, and sudden flight. Time after time, he lured U.S. and Mexican soldiers into deadly ambushes. The killings and raids on both sides of the border surpassed anything previously experienced in Apache raids. In 14 months, Victorio may have killed as many as a thousand whites and Mexicans. He attacked wagon trains, stole livestock, and murdered ranch families. One of the only surviving members of Victorio's band remembered, "I do not like to think of the things I witnessed."

In October 1880, while moving along the Rio Grande, Victorio and his band were surrounded and wiped out by Mexican soldiers at Cerro Tres Castillos. The Mexicans killed and scalped 78 Apache and paraded the scalps on poles into Chihuahua. The Mexicans also captured 68 women and children. Only 17 Apaches, including women and children, escaped.

A LOW-STATUS PROFESSION

Americans had long distrusted professional soldiers and a standing army. They had rebelled against England for this very reason.

In America, a military career was often considered a last resort for people who could not do anything else. The Civil War had changed things, glorifying the role of the heroic soldier. But no sooner did it

Nana's Raid

Nana (c. 1800–1896) was Geronimo's brother-in-law. He was one of the only Apache to escape the destruction of Victorio's band. Nana gathered the few remaining warriors and led them to hidden places in the Sierra Madre to rest and recuperate. Even though he was now about 80 years old, Nana swore he would revenge the disaster at Tres Castillos. One member of his group remembered that Nana "was not content with an eye for an eye, nor a life for a life. For every Apache killed he took many lives."

Although Nana appeared feeble and limped perceptibly, his endurance was legendary. To his people, he was a wise, kind, grandfatherly figure. He was considerate to women, friendly to the young, courteous to fellow warriors, and completely devoted to his tribe. However, his hatred of whites was boundless.

In the summer of 1881, Nana began a series of slashing raids through the mountains of southern New Mexico. Although old and crippled, he rode as much as 70 miles (112 km) a day. Nana's band attacked army units and citizen's posses, killing miners, herders, Mexican-Americans, every person he encountered. Eight companies of cavalry, eight companies of infantry, and two companies of Indian Scouts were assigned to run him down, but Nana's band inflicted casualties and melted away unharmed. "Nana's Raid" is arguably the most brilliant deed of war ever performed by the Chiricahua.

In the end, Nana's group of about 15 warriors covered more than a thousand miles (1,609 km)—an average of 50 miles (80 km) a day. They fought seven serious battles with cavalry and won every one. They killed 50 Americans and stole hundreds of cattle and horses. By the end of 1881, Nana's Raid was over and his group slipped back into Sonora. Despite being outnumbered 10-to-1, the 80-year-old warrior had gained some revenge for Victorio's defeat and death.

end, than the military was dismantled. At the end of the Civil War, the Union Army numbered 200,000 men. In 1866, the U.S. government reduced the regular army to 56,000 men, most stationed in the South to enforce Reconstruction. In 1869, the army was reduced to 45,000 men; to 30,000 men in 1870; and to 25,000 men in 1874. (In 2009, the U.S. military totaled close to 3 million people.)

All of the men in this Indian-fighting army were volunteers who had enlisted for a five-year term. The average age for soldiers was 23. Many were recent immigrants and most were poor. Many were attracted by the steady employment offered by the army, with its pay of $13 per month for privates, regular rations, and free medical care. Some joined for adventure in the American West. Others were just rootless veterans of the Civil War who had lost everything or former slaves who had nothing to start. The military also attracted criminals who found it useful to travel where they could not be traced.

Soldiering was difficult, especially in the dreary frontier outposts of the Southwest. Desertion was the most common crime in the army. In an 1891 report, the Secretary of War reported that losses through desertion between 1867 and 1891 averaged one-third of all enlistees. Some people joined the army just to get free transportation to the goldfields of the west, where they would promptly desert.

The basic army unit was the company. After 1876, each company was supposed to have 100 privates, but most were understrength. Companies were self-contained social as well as military units. A soldier had little contact with men outside his company. He was completely at the mercy of his noncommissioned officers, usually men of long service. He could not even speak to an officer without the permission of the first sergeant, who actually ran the company.

A wide gulf separated enlisted men from their commissioned officers. Most officers came from the upper class of society and graduated from United States Military Academy at West Point. Many officers, assigned to a post in what he considered "the end of the world," found no friends and the duty dull. Alcoholism was a constant problem, contributing to the public impression that soldiering was a low-status profession.

ANOTHER BREAKOUT

By 1880, Geronimo was about 55 years old. People described him as a powerful and stocky man, about 5 foot 8 inches (172 cm) and 170 pounds (77 kg). He was shorter than Cochise and Mangas Coloradas, but taller than the average Chiricahua warrior, who stood 5 foot 6 inches (167.5 cm) and weighed about 135 pounds (61.2 kg).

Geronimo lived at San Carlos for about a year. Despite the close ties between Victorio's people and those of Geronimo and Juh, the two groups did not join forces. The two Chiricahua leaders were living on the reservation at the time of Nana's Raid. Yet even though they stayed out of it, they were affected by the panic of U.S. government officials.

In 1881, an Apache mystic named Nochedelklinne began making wild prophecies. He predicted that all whites would soon disappear and the dead Apache chiefs would return to life. He taught the Apache to do a circle dance, known as the Ghost Dance, which included trances, prophesizing, and wild dancing. The reservation Apache flocked to him and danced with a religious ecstasy that frightened white observers. Even the skeptical Geronimo visited the prophet and wondered about the truth of his predictions.

This emotional upheaval at San Carlos took place at the same time that Nana was terrorizing southern New Mexico. The Americans in charge of the reservation were understandably nervous. However, they did not come up with the correct solution. In August 1881, the corrupt Indian agent Joseph Tiffany told Colonel Eugene Carr, the commander at Fort Apache, that he wanted Nochedelklinne "arrested or killed or both." When Carr arrested Nochedelklinne, a riot broke out. The prophet, about 18 Apache, and 8 of Carr's men were killed at Cibecue Creek. Geronimo was probably not present at this tragic incident.

The Apache were justifiably enraged by Nochedelklinne's arrest and death. However, the white Southwest was unnerved by Nana's

Pictured are Apache chiefs (*left to right*) Chihuahua, Naiche, Loco, Nana, and Geronimo. This photograph was taken around 1890.

Raid and the fear of a general Apache breakout from the reservation. As a precaution, the army poured large numbers of troops into San Carlos.

The Chiricahua feared the army troops. "A rumor was current that the officers were again planning to imprison our leaders," remembered Geronimo. "This rumor served to revive the memory of all our past wrongs—the massacre in the tent at Apache Pass, the fate of Mangas Coloradas, and my own unjust imprisonment...." When the military requested Geronimo's presence for the conference at Fort Thomas, the Chiricahua leader and his warriors feared treachery. "We thought it more manly to die on the warpath than to be killed in prison," he said.

And so, in September of 1881, Geronimo and some followers bolted the San Carlos reservation. With them was Naiche, Cochise's younger son and the hereditary chief of the Chiricahua after Taza's death in 1876. On the way to the border, the fugitives killed everyone they met, picking up supplies and horses as they fled. The army pursued them, attacking them twice in inconclusive actions, but failed to stop them.

Geronimo's trail took him close to Tombstone, Arizona. Mayor John Clum, still filled with his hatred for Geronimo, led a posse to catch him, including three of the famous Earp brothers. (The famous shootout at OK Corral would take place the next month.) However, no one could catch the speeding Apache warriors. They were soon safely across the border in the Sierra Madre of Mexico. In the end, Geronimo and his warriors chose open hostility over the uncertainty of San Carlos life.

6

RENEGADE

In October 1881, Geronimo, Juh, and about 250 followers returned to full-time raiding activities from a camp in the Sierra Madre Mountains. Mexico, however, was no longer a safe refuge for the Apache. According to Geronimo, the "Mexicans were gathering troops in the mountains where we had been ranging, and their numbers were so much greater than ours that we could not hope to fight them successfully, and we were tired of being chased about from place to place." The Apache had good American guns but not enough ammunition.

Juh and Geronimo concocted a bold plan. In the spring of 1882, they decided to raid the San Carlos Reservation and convince the remaining Warm Springs Apache to accompany them back to Mexico. To cross the border, reach San Carlos, and return without detection was not easy. In one incident, Geronimo's war party came upon a sheep ranch about 20 miles (32 km) north of Safford, Arizona. In cold blood, they murdered the foreman, his wife, two children, ten Mexican herders, and the other women who cooked the meals. Actions like these soon spread Geronimo's reputation among white Americans as a subhuman monster.

"I do not think that he wanted to kill," remembered a young member of Geronimo's band. "If he were seen by a civilian, it meant that he would be reported to the military and they'd be after us, so there was nothing to do but kill the civilian and his entire family. It was terrible to see little children killed.... There were times that I hated Geronimo for that, too; but when I got older, I knew that he had no choice." Certainly, he could be merciless when it came to killing Mexicans.

At San Carlos, Geronimo's band had to virtually kidnap the Warm Springs Apache, now under Loco after Victorio's death. Many of Loco's people at San Carlos, especially the women and children, did not want to leave the reservation to be hunted by the Mexicans and the Americans. Loco was a brave warrior but he believed the struggle was useless and that continued fighting would only lead to extermination. Geronimo's nephew said, "And so far as I know, nobody was critical of Loco. The great Cochise had felt the same way. All of us knew that we were doomed, but some preferred death to slavery and imprisonment."

Naiche, the son of Cochise, was now the official chief of the Chiricahua. However, one Warm Springs Apache noted that "Geronimo was pretty much the main leader although he was not the born chief of any band.... But Geronimo seemed to be the most intelligent and resourceful as well as the most vigorous and farsighted."

Geronimo, Juh, Loco, and the large group of about 100 warriors and 300 women and children now made a dash to the border. The ranging war parties killed more than 50 people—prospectors, wagon train drivers, ranchers, lone travelers, everyone they met on their raids. They knew this would stir up the soldiers but they felt they had no choice. "Even babies were killed; and I love babies," remembered one Apache. "But Geronimo was fighting not only to avenge his murdered mother, wife, and children, but for his people and his tribe."

The large Apache band fled Arizona with incredible skill. When they crossed the border, they assumed they were safe and relaxed their guard. However, unknown to them, the U.S. troops had decided to disregard international law and cross the border. At Sierra Emmedio, a small mountain in Chihuahua, the American soldiers attacked the Apache while they were celebrating their escape. The Chiricahua managed to hold off their attackers, but at the cost of 14 warriors and almost all their supplies, which they left behind when they fled the camp.

Advancing further into Mexico, the Apache were then caught in an ambush by Mexican troops at Aliso Creek. After a brutal

Naiche, the youngest son of Cochise, was the last chief of the free Chiricahua. Initially he was cooperative with whites, leading his people to surrender to General Howard and settle at San Carlos in 1876. A few years later, however, Naiche fled the reservation and rode with Geronimo with small groups of warriors on several raids in Arizona and Mexico.

skirmish, Apache warriors fled in all directions. Eleven warriors and more than 60 Apache women and children were killed; 19 Mexican soldiers also died.

Geronimo's plan to kidnap Loco's people had cost the Apache dearly. About 25 warriors (out of about 100) and many of Loco's women and children lay dead. On the other hand, the Chiricahua bands had temporarily reunited in one camp. They still had experienced warriors, and they felt secure in their mountain refuge.

LIFE IN THE SIERRA MADRE

The "wild" Apache peoples, now numbering several hundred, used the Sierra Madre as a base to make raiding expeditions in Mexico. Occasionally, Geronimo slipped across the border into Arizona and New Mexico to steal much-needed ammunition.

The Apache sometimes traded the spoils of their raids in the markets of Casas Grandes. On one occasion, Mexicans attacked the Apache after the Natives got drunk in Casas Grandes. "We fled in all directions," remembered Geronimo. The Mexicans killed about 20 Apache and captured 30 women and children. Among those captured was Cheehashkish, Geronimo's wife and the mother of his teenaged son and daughter. He never saw her again. Sometime after this, Geronimo married Ziyeh, who would survive to share his captivity.

For the next year, the Apache plundered Mexican villages, stole cattle, horses, and mules, and captured pack trains. The women stayed hidden in the mountains where they dried beef, gathered and stored wild plants, and made clothing from material stolen by their men. The Apache had enough to eat, good clothing, and no nearby enemies. There were soldiers in Mexican towns but the raiding parties either avoided them or drove them off. The Mexicans did not dare attempt to hunt the Apache out of the mountains.

It was a good life, since the Apache did not concern themselves with the feelings of the Mexicans. Geronimo still hated everyone in the state of Sonora for the massacre of his family. He did not care how many Mexicans suffered, or whether they were innocent or guilty.

Still, the Chiricahua, now numbering almost 600, could not stay united for long. The bands followed too many different leaders and held too many differing opinions and old grudges. An Apache warrior was not a soldier but a free man. He could come and go as he wanted and make his own decisions. Soon the large group broke up into smaller units.

    One of these subgroups, led by Chatto and Chihuahua, raided Arizona in March 1883. The raiders covered 400 miles (643 km) in 6 days, stealing horses and killing 26 people while losing only one warrior. However, the raid was to have fateful consequences. The raiders unknowingly killed a federal judge and his wife and kidnapped their son. The murders and kidnapping threw the entire border country into an uproar and received national headlines. Pressure mounted in Mexico and the United States to do something about the hostile Apache at large in the Sierra Madre.

CROOK'S RETURN

In September 1882, General George Crook returned to the Southwest to resume his position as commander of the Department of Arizona. He was still a mass of contradictions. He believed that the greed and the stupidity of the U.S. government and army caused almost all American Indian problems. "All the tribes tell the same story. They are surrounded on all sides, the game is destroyed or driven away, they are left to starve, and there remains but one thing for them to do—fight while they can," wrote Crook. "Some people think the Indians do not understand these things, but they do, and fully appreciate the circumstances in which they are placed."

    Yet, as an army general, Crook did his best to annihilate the Apache. The Chiricahua "are an incorrigible lot," Crook wrote, "the worst band of Indians in America. . . . [I] should be glad to learn that the last of the Chiricahuas was under ground."

    Crook discovered the location of Geronimo's base camp in Mexico by a stroke of luck. An Apache warrior had deserted Chatto, returned to the reservation, and acted as the general's guide. Crook then asked for and received Mexican permission to cross the international border. This was technically an armed invasion of Mexico, but both countries were becoming desperate. They felt they had to cooperate if they wanted to subdue the Apache bands.

Crook chose his force carefully: 9 officers, 42 enlisted men, and 193 Apache scouts. In May 1883, the Apache scouts working for the U.S. Army surprised Geronimo's mountain hideout while the warriors were away raiding. They looted the camp, rounded up the horses, and captured five children. Over the next few days, the soldiers convinced many of the hostile Apache to surrender with a promise that they could return to the reservation.

Geronimo arrived at the camp five days after its capture. Following several conferences with Crook, he also agreed to return to San Carlos with most of the other hostile Chiricahua, including Nana and Loco. Only Juh (who would die of a heart attack in November) did not offer to surrender.

Crook returned to Arizona with about 50 warriors and 270 women and children. Most were glad to return to the reservation, even if it was San Carlos. One Apache said that it was "a great relief to give up to superior authority.... No more worries, no more sleepless nights, fearing attack by an enemy." Naiche, Chihuahua, and about another 100 Apache returned to San Carlos in the late fall. By the end of November, more than 400 "hostiles," including about 80 warriors, were on the reservation.

However, the situation was unstable. Some of the returning Apache were happy to give up the fugitive life. Others believed that their surrender was only the temporary result of the discovery of their mountain stronghold. They hoped to break out again in the spring. On the other hand, many white Arizonans demanded all the Chiricahua men be executed, the women distributed to other tribes, and the land given to European-Americans.

APACHE SCOUTS

Indian agent John Clum had used Apache to police the reservation. They provided "very effective assistance in maintaining order," he

Renegade 71

Under the leadership of General George Crook, a group of Apache scouts hunted down Geronimo and brought him back to San Carlos Reservation. Pictured is the cover of a newspaper showing White Mountain Apache scouts at a Southern Pacific Railway Station on the plains. In the box is an illustration of Geronimo.

said, as well as serving as guards and spies. General Crook took the idea one step further. Crook knew enough about the terrain of the Southwest to understand that American soldiers were no match for Apache guerrilla warriors. He decided that the best trackers of Apache were other Apache.

In 1871, Crook recruited 75 Western Apache as scouts for the U.S. Army. For the next 15 years, these Apache scouts pursued bands of Chiricahua Apache throughout most of the Arizona Territory and finally into Mexico. To command them, Crook selected some of the finest officers in his department, quiet and modest field soldiers such as Emmet Crawford, Britton Davis, and Charles Gatewood.

Recruitment for the Apache scouts was not difficult because great hatreds existed among the various bands. A few of the scouts were Chiricahua but most of them belonged to other reservation tribes unfriendly to the raiders. For the Western Apache, Geronimo had always meant trouble. Although the Chiricahua and Western Apache spoke related languages and shared a similar culture, they had separate homelands and did not like each other.

These divisions played into Crook's hands. He knew that not all Apache people were alike. The various bands lacked any central leadership and did not see their common interest. Crook later noted that the Apache "don't fear the white soldiers, whom they easily surpass in the peculiar style of warfare which they force upon us, but put upon their trail an enemy of their own blood, an enemy as tireless, as foxy, and as stealthy and familiar with the country as they themselves, and it breaks them all up.... Nothing has ever been accomplished without [the scout's] help."

By 1885, most Apache did not want to join the "renegades." They understood the army's overwhelming advantage in numbers and weapons. One Mescalero Apache said, "The scouts made friends with the whites and knew what life was like. They knew it was best to surrender." Many strongly disagreed with the warriors who kept fighting. They blamed Geronimo and the other "hostiles" for the death and devastation inflicted on the whole band. For warriors on the reservation, scouting for the U.S. Army was one of the only ways to follow the traditional life of a warrior.

Yet Crook's idea of Apache scouts was shockingly radical in its time. For most white Arizonans, the only good American Indian was a dead American Indian. Now Crook was hiring Apache to do the work of American soldiers. The *Silver City Enterprise* editorialized, "The general's great hobby is his Apache scouts.... Who are these scouts? Why they are mostly Apache Indians, friends and relatives of Geronimo's band.... In reality, the Indians are about the ugliest and filthiest brutes on the globe—lying, thieving, gambling cut throats ... " The editorial ended by calling for a massacre if the government refused to remove every last Apache from Arizona.

TURKEY CREEK

In June 1883, Crook had granted Geronimo permission to stay a few more days to gather the rest of his scattered people before returning to San Carlos. Geronimo thought about staying in Mexico but he was almost out of ammunition. Nonetheless, he stayed out until February 1884. When he finally appeared at San Carlos, he brought his three wives and children, along with 26 warriors and about 70 women and children. He also brought 135 head of cattle that he had stolen from Mexicans and, in turn, were confiscated by General Crook. The confiscation of the cattle particularly bothered Geronimo, and he complained about it the rest of his life.

The recently hostile Apache settled down at San Carlos in 1884 and 1885. There were some honest attempts by white Americans to deal with the Apache fairly. Crook allowed the Apache to settle wherever they wanted, and Geronimo's band chose Turkey Creek, about 17 miles (27.3 km) southeast of Fort Apache. It was a beautiful region of tall pines, clear streams, lots of game, and a perfect summer climate. The area did not contain enough farmland or water for irrigation, however. This was a problem, since the Department of the Interior insisted on trying to convert the Chiricahua into farmers.

The Apache now numbered 521, of whom 127 were men and boys capable of bearing arms. Most were satisfied with their new home site. "There was an abundance of good water, wood, and

Geronimo and his people settled at Turkey Creek and began farming. Although the nomads were used to roaming throughout the Southwest unrestrained, hunting game and finding fruit, berries, nuts, and herbs, they tried to make the best of their situation. Above, Apache men dig irrigation ditches under military supervision.

game. There was good grazing. There were no mosquitoes, few rattlesnakes, and no cavalry. There were poles and brush to make shelters, and even the canvas of old tents for covering until hides could be secured." They generally liked Britton Davis, the young lieutenant in charge of the Apache scouts. They thought he was honest and fair, and treated them as individuals.

The more Davis dealt with the Chiricahua, the more he sympathized with them. "In treachery, broken pledges on the part of high officials, lies, thievery, slaughter of defenseless women and children, and every crime in the catalogue of man's inhumanity to man the Indian was a mere amateur compared to the 'noble white man.' His crimes were retail, ours wholesale," Davis said.

Some problems remained. At San Carlos, General Crook had banned two traditional Apache practices: the production of tizwin and the right of men to beat their adulterous wives. Crook especially feared that tizwin drinking caused disorder and violence. The Apache complained that since the Americans and Mexicans drank "to make them feel good," why should they forbid the Apache from drinking? And who were the white men to tell them how to run their culture? They had not come into the reservation to be told what to do.

In 1884, the reservation raised an estimated 45,000 pounds (about 20,400 kilograms) of corn, a considerable amount of barley, and many melons, pumpkins, and other vegetables. The Chiricahua gathered wild food, killed deer, dried venison, and tanned skins for clothing and wickiup covers. Except for their constant fear of betrayal, they had a good summer. When the fall came, the Apache held a big dance and feast to celebrate the end of the season. Then, they moved their camps down to the lower altitudes in a valley of the White River near Fort Apache.

The former "hostiles" loyally observed the peace made with Crook in the Sierra Madre almost two years before. There had not been one act of Apache violence in all the Southwest in 1884. Crook noted in his 1884 report that, "for the first time in the history of the fierce people, every member of the Apache tribe is at peace."

THE LAST BREAKOUT

Things seemed to be going well for the Chiricahua at San Carlos, but many of the young warriors were edgy. The sudden arrest and imprisonment of the Apache warrior Kaytennae angered them. They disliked the intrusions and rules of whites, especially the law against making tizwin. There were constant rumors of impending trials and hangings.

On May 17, 1885, Geronimo, Naiche, and Nana fled San Carlos with about three dozen warriors and 100 women and children. However, three-quarters of the band had refused to leave the reservation, including Loco and Chatto. They were not cowards. They just felt they could never hope to defeat the Americans, and they could not hide forever in the Sierra Madre.

Geronimo was the main instigator behind this breakout. He later wrote, "General Crook ordered officers, soldiers, and scouts to see that I was arrested; if I offered resistance they were instructed to kill me." This was a reasonable fear; Mangas Coloradas and Nochedelklinne suffered a similar fate, and later, so did Crazy Horse and Sitting Bull. However, such an action would be out of General Crook's character and was probably just rumor. Geronimo admitted, "This information was brought to me by the Indians. When I learned of this proposed action I left for Old Mexico..."

The Apache did have good reason to be distrustful of the Americans. Nonetheless, Geronimo's nervousness probably crossed the line into paranoia. This would be his fourth breakout from a reservation, not including the kidnapping of Loco. Geronimo's suspicions that the Americans would murder him now became a major motivating factor for his actions.

The hostile Apaches killed 17 civilians as they dashed to the Mexican border. They traveled 120 miles (193 km) without pausing to rest or eat. Twenty troops of cavalry and 200 Apache scouts crisscrossed the mountains, watched the border, guarded the water holes, and followed every trail, but to no avail. Geronimo's small band eluded all their pursuers.

The flight of Geronimo caused panic across southern Arizona and New Mexico. "Apaches on Warpath" headlined newspapers. Sensationalized press reports exaggerated Geronimo's activities, making him the most feared Apache in both countries. Yet there were only about 40 Apache warriors in a territory the size of all of New England.

THE BUFFALO SOLDIERS

Geronimo regularly used the term "white man" as a synonym for "Americans." In the same way, many historians freely use the term "white people" to describe Geronimo's adversaries. However, some of the Apache's fiercest opponents had dark skin.

African-American soldiers had fought in the Revolution and the War of 1812 and 200,000 had served in the Civil War. Some black soldiers wanted to remain in the army after 1865. These men were organized into the 9th and 10th Cavalry regiments. For the next 20 years, these "Buffalo Soldiers" battled Native Americans from Montana to Arizona.

The reason for the name Buffalo Soldiers is uncertain. It is possible that Native tribes were comparing the black soldiers' hair to the mane of a buffalo. Another view is that a wounded buffalo will fight

Buffalo Soldiers participated in many military campaigns against the American Indians. Ironically, although Buffalo Soldiers worked for the U.S. Army, black men were still not accepted and were made to live in tents in Rhyolite Canyon, closer to the danger of hostile bands of Apache, although Fort Bowie was less than a day's ride away by horse. Above, a stagecoach is guarded by Buffalo Soldiers at a relay station.

ferociously and courageously. Either way, the name was probably an honor, since the Plains tribes held the buffalo in such high regard.

The Buffalo Soldiers regularly battled the Apache in the Southwest. They fought against Geronimo and Juh's groups in 1876–1877. For more than a year in 1879–1880, they waged a grueling campaign to catch Victorio's raiders, pursuing the Apache chief over thousands of miles. They also served in the last campaign against Geronimo in 1885–1886. When not fighting the Apache, the Buffalo Soldiers built forts and roads, installed telegraph lines, guarded water holes, escorted wagon trains, and protected stagecoaches.

While individual black soldiers might have sympathized with the Apache, the Buffalo Soldiers were employed to fight Native Americans and protect white settlements. The Buffalo Soldiers and their officers did not make American Indian policy; they carried it out, regardless of merit, to the best of their ability.

"ONCE I MOVED ABOUT LIKE THE WIND"

The U.S. Army marshaled all its resources to capture Geronimo's band, no matter which side of the border they were on. In summer 1885, two large forces of American soldiers, close to 3,000 men, entered Mexico to search for Geronimo in the Sierra Madre. They attacked Geronimo's camp in August, capturing fifteen women, including two of Geronimo's wives, and five of his children.

They did not hurt him enough to prevent an autumn Apache raid into the United States. This raid, led by Ulzana, was the last of its kind. From November 23 to the end of 1885, the 12 raiders covered 1,200 miles (1,931 km), killed 38 people, and captured 250 head of livestock with just a single casualty. The raid inflamed settlers and prompted the army's commander in chief, Phil Sheridan, to journey from Washington, D.C., to meet with General Crook at Fort Bowie.

Geronimo killed Mexicans because he liked to see them die; however, killing Americans was a part of raiding for supplies. In an 1890 interview, Crook asked Naiche why they killed people. The chief answered, "Because we were afraid. It was war. Anyone who saw us would kill us, and we did the same thing. We had to if we wanted to live."

Finally, in January 1886, Crook's Apache scouts discovered and attacked the remote Chiricahua camp in Mexico. Geronimo and his followers escaped but they lost nearly everything in the camp to Crook's soldiers, including their horses and precious supplies. The American soldiers captured many of the wives and children of the warriors. This was a blow to morale; the warriors could not see the point of fighting if they could never see their families again.

Cold, hungry, and discouraged, Geronimo and Nana were ready to talk surrender terms with General Crook. They met for three days beginning March 25 at Cañon de los Embudos, just

General George Crook (*third from right*) holds council with Geronimo (*center left*) at a three-day conference at Cañon de los Embudos, in the Sierra Madre. Crook was unsuccessful in persuading Geronimo to surrender and return to the San Carlos Reservation. This photo was taken by Tucson photographer C.S. Fly.

south of the American border. Tucson photographer C.S. Fly took an amazing series of photographs of the defiant Apache warriors and their meeting with Crook. On the third day of negotiations, Geronimo agreed to return with Crook's force. "Once I moved about like the wind," Geronimo told the general. "Now I surrender to you and that is all."

Crook's orders were to get an unconditional surrender with no promises made to the Apache "unless it is necessary to secure their surrender." Crook interpreted this to mean that failing to secure an unconditional surrender, he was to make the best terms possible. Crook's agreement with Geronimo was that the Apache would be imprisoned for two years in the East and then settled on a reservation in their homeland.

Phil Sheridan, Crook's superior officer, later voided that agreement. Sheridan claimed that a reservation in Arizona was impossible; the Apache should be thankful their lives were spared. To Crook's dishonor, he never told his Apache prisoners that the terms had been revoked, even though he already knew it while traveling with the Apache back to Arizona.

For Geronimo, the agreement turned out to be moot, anyway. He shook hands with Crook on the deal but the Chiricahua warrior did not honor his pledge. A trader supplied the ever-suspicious Geronimo with liquor, and the drinking began. Again, some of the Apache began to fear that they would be taken to a place worse than San Carlos where they would all die of disease. Maybe the Americans would jail them or hang them when they crossed the border? That night, Geronimo, Naiche, and 45 others—about half women and children—slipped out of camp.

Years later, Geronimo explained, "We started with all our tribe to go with General Crook back to the United States, but I feared treachery and decided to remain in Mexico. We were not under any guard at this time. The United States troops marched in front and the Indians followed, and when we became suspicious, we turned back."

The Apache wars had not yet ended.

THE LAST CAMPAIGN

Geronimo's escape would have vast implications for his chief adversary. General Crook received such harsh criticism for allowing Geronimo to escape that he was forced to resign. His use of the Apache scouts particularly irritated Phil Sheridan, who appointed General Nelson Miles to replace Crook as head of the Department of Arizona.

Miles was an experienced American Indian fighter with a tendency to self-glorification. He had fought bravely in many major battles of the Civil War, including Antietam, Chancellorsville, the Wilderness, and Spotsylvania. He was wounded four times, once seriously, and rose to the rank of major general of volunteers by age

26. The pomp and ceremony of army life appealed to Miles, and he decided to make it a career. After the Civil War, he fought against the Kiowa, Comanche, Cheyenne, Sioux, and Nez Percé.

Miles came to Arizona with great ambitions. He wanted to become a major general or maybe even president. Crook and Miles were rivals who detested each other but they had some things in common. Like Crook, Miles believed all his fellow officers were incompetent. Both men could carry a long grudge when they felt they were insulted.

The Apache had no respect for Miles. One warrior said, "If Crook was disliked, you should know how much more bitterly Miles was hated; he was regarded as a coward, a liar, and a poor officer.... In comparison to Crook, he was despicable."

Miles rejected Crook's reliance on Apache scouts and dismissed almost all of them. Instead, Miles used more than 5,000 soldiers, one-quarter of the entire army, to catch 37 Chiricahua: 18 warriors, 13 women, and 6 children. In addition, another 3,000 Mexican soldiers were in the field to track down Geronimo's band.

Yet despite the efforts of handpicked units that remained in the field for months, Miles's men did not capture a single Apache, not even a child. For more than five months, the Chiricahua ran the soldiers ragged. Throughout the blistering Sierra Madre summer of 1886, Geronimo's tiny band eluded the soldiers sent out to capture him. This astonishing feat of cunning and endurance cemented Geronimo's reputation as a master strategist and charismatic leader.

Geronimo's band had no one to help them and no place to go. Hounded constantly, they knew the situation was hopeless. Geronimo baldly stated, "On our return through Old Mexico we attacked every Mexican found, even if for no other reason than to kill. We believed they had asked the United States troops to come down to Mexico to fight us.... We gave no quarter to anyone and asked no favors."

"Geronimo had to obtain food for his men, and for their women and children," remembered Kanseah, an 11-year-old boy in that last band. "When they were hungry, Geronimo got food. When they

The Woman Warrior

Women occupied an honored and secure place in Apache society. Nonetheless, like women in most preindustrial groups, their life choices were extremely limited. In a story of a warrior people, the women of the tribe are noticeably missing.

Victorio's sister, Lozen [c.1848–c. 1890] is the exception. Although some women did fight, Lozen was memorialized as "The Woman Warrior." She refused all offers of marriage in order to fight as a warrior, riding along with the men. Lozen was an excellent shot, an expert at roping, and was especially skilled at stealing horses. "Lozen is as my right hand," Victorio told his sub-chiefs. "Strong as a man, braver than most, and cunning in strategy, Lozen is a shield to her people."

Lozen was most respected for her unique power. She alone among the band had the ability to locate the enemy. She could even tell how far away the enemy was. To Victorio's misfortune, she was out on a mission when his band was ambushed at Tres Castillos. She then joined up with Geronimo until his final surrender in 1886. Geronimo recognized her bravery and used her on missions to the American military officers to arrange for meetings. She died of illness in captivity in Alabama.

---

were cold, he provided blankets and clothing. When they were afoot, he stole horses. When they had no bullets, he got ammunition. He was a good man."

Miles selected Captain Henry Lawton to lead the expedition to capture Geronimo. Lawton's men marched 1,600 miles (2,574 km) in four months but never succeeded in closing with the Chiricahua and did not kill or capture a single hostile.

In frustration, Miles made a fateful decision. He decided to proceed against some Apache he could find—the 400 men, women, and children who had remained at peace on the reservation. Many of them had served as Apache scouts for the U.S. Army and had never been disarmed. Their leaders included Loco, Chatto, and

Kaytennae, all of whom had led raids in the past but who had also helped fight Geronimo. For no particular reason, Miles decided to move these peaceful Chiricahua from San Carlos to prison in Florida. They had not joined Geronimo's breakout, but they would still be prisoners of war.

SURRENDER?

Geronimo's band was mentally exhausted from fleeing through northern Mexico. However, they never thought about surrendering until Charles Gatewood and two Chiricahua Apache scouts (Martine and Kayitah) approached them. Miles had sent them to find Geronimo and to try to negotiate peace terms. Miles's dreams of glory were starting to crumble; if Geronimo's band remained at large much longer, his career and reputation might be fatally tarnished.

Miles's choice of Gatewood was particularly astute. George Wratten wrote that Geronimo "always had great faith in Lieutenant Gatewood, for he had never deceived him. He was the only man who could safely have gotten within gun shot of the old savage, and General Miles knew that when he sent him out." Led by the two brave scouts, Gatewood made his way to Geronimo's camp in the Sierra Madre.

Geronimo and Naiche told Gatewood they wanted to return to San Carlos, and there should be no civil trials in Arizona for any crimes they had committed since they left. Instead, Gatewood told him, "Surrender, and you will be sent to join the rest of your people in Florida, there to await the decision of the President as to your final disposition. Accept these terms or fight it out to the bitter end." Geronimo initially refused Gatewood's surrender proposition and decided to fight to the last man. Geronimo said that to surrender the whole "Southwest to a race of intruders" was too much for Miles to demand.

Gatewood then played his last card. He told Geronimo that a return to San Carlos was impossible because every one of the 400 Chiricahua and Warm Springs Apache were to be removed to

Florida. There would be no Chiricahua or Warm Springs Apache left in Arizona and only their traditional enemies would inhabit San Carlos.

General Nelson Miles used different tactics from General Crook to try to capture Geronimo. Instead of using Apache scouts, Miles assembled 5,000 U.S. troops to patrol the Mexican border and guard all watering holes. His best decision was to send Lieutenant Charles Gatewood to negotiate with Geronimo.

The hostiles were shocked that the Apache on the reservation had been sent as prisoners to Florida. All the fight drained out of them. What was the point of continuing if the reservation was gone and their families were in Florida? Gatewood wrote his wife, "They are tired of fighting and want to be united with their families once more.... Can anyone blame a man for wanting to see his wife and children?" After asking whether General Miles was trustworthy, Geronimo agreed to surrender on the condition that the Apache would be immediately reunited with their families. At the end, his group consisted of only 18 warriors, 12 women, and 6 children.

The little band of Apache began walking back to the United States to meet with General Miles. The glory-seeking Miles kept his distance. He did not want to have anything to do with Geronimo's band unless he was sure they were going to surrender. Then he could call himself "the man who had captured Geronimo." However, if the Apache were going to flee into the mountains, Miles wanted to be far enough away to escape the fate of General Crook. Miles got so nervous, he strongly suggested to Lawton that he murder Geronimo in cold blood and solve the problem.

SKELETON CANYON

The two adversaries finally met at Skeleton Canyon in the Peloncillo Range on the Arizona–New Mexico border on September 3, 1886. Miles was impressed with Geronimo: "He was one of the brightest, most resolute, determined looking men that I have ever encountered. He had the clearest, sharpest, dark eye I think I have ever seen.... Every movement indicated power, energy, and determination. In everything he did he had a purpose."

The interpreter told Geronimo that "General Miles was his friend." Geronimo responded, "I never saw him, but I have been in need of friends. Why has he not been with me?" When this was interpreted, general laughter broke out among the officers and a lot of the tension went out of the meeting.

Miles seemed to agree with Gatewood's terms that the Chiricahua would eventually be resettled on a reservation in Arizona after an undetermined imprisonment. Miles said, "Lay down your arms and come with me to Fort Bowie, and in five days you will see your families now in Florida with Chihuahua, and no harm will be done you." Certainly, Geronimo believed that the Chiricahua would be pardoned by the government of their so-called crimes and eventually be granted a reservation in their homeland. Years later, when he was an old man, Geronimo would relate how he still "looked in vain for General Miles to send me to that land of which he had spoken; I longed in vain for the implements, house, and stock that General Miles had promised me."

On the way to Fort Bowie, Geronimo looked out on his beloved Chiricahua Mountains and remarked, "This is the fourth time I have surrendered." Miles quickly answered, "And I think it is the last time." Strictly speaking, Geronimo had not been captured but induced by false promises to surrender. As one warrior said, "Nobody ever captured Geronimo. I know. I was with him. Anyway, who can capture the wind?"

8

LIVING LEGEND

"That day they put us on the train at Bowie, Arizona, would have been a good day to die," remembered one young Apache warrior. "Banishment from our land and the bones of our ancestors was worse than death.... We knew that we were facing two years of slavery and degradation, [but we were] willing to endure that for the sake of the future when we were to be free again." No one knew the Apache would be prisoners for 27 years.

Geronimo and his band were probably lucky at that. Most of the white citizens of Arizona wanted the hostiles hanged without further ado. In fact, President Grover Cleveland telegraphed the War Department, "I hope nothing will be done with Geronimo which will prevent our keeping him as a prisoner of war, if we cannot hang him, which I would much prefer."

Such a betrayal even exceeded General Miles's capacity for double-dealing, however. Miles at least made sure that Geronimo and his people made it out of Arizona without being lynched. In the end, the women and children joined the other Chiricahua captives at Fort Marion in St. Augustine, Florida, while Geronimo, Naiche, and the other hostiles were sent to Fort Pickens in Pensacola, Florida.

Geronimo and the remaining Apache, including scouts who had been assigned to track him down and Chiricahuas who had been living peacefully at San Carlos, were sent to Fort Pickens in Pensacola, Florida. In this 1886 photo, Apache are en route to their imprisonment in Florida. Geronimo is third from right in the front row.

So the Chiricahua families were separated even though that was the main reason that Geronimo's band had surrendered. Not that it mattered, but General D.S. Stanley reported that the Chiricahua "regarded the separation of themselves from their families as a violation of the terms of their treaty of surrender..."

The trip to Florida was a nightmare. The Apache crossed the Southwest in a train with all the doors and windows fastened shut. The heat was intense and the living conditions filthy. The prisoners feared they would be murdered at any moment.

THE BETRAYAL OF THE APACHE

Almost 400 Chiricahua prisoners of war reached Florida in the fall of 1886, most of whom had stayed peacefully on the reservation while Geronimo was out raiding. This number included the Apache scouts, who amazingly were still working for and receiving pay from the U.S. Army.

This was the most peculiar part of the government's policy. The Apache scouts who had served so loyally went to the same jail as the renegades. The U.S. Army imprisoned Chatto and the other Chiricahua who had helped them just as if they had been with Geronimo to the end. Martine and Kayitah, the two loyal scouts who had made the surrender possible, were shipped on the same train that carried Geronimo's band to Florida. General Crook's chief aide was astonished. He wrote, "There is no more disgraceful page in the history of our relations with the American Indians than that which conceals the treachery visited upon the Chiricahua who remained faithful in their allegiance" to the Americans.

The Chiricahua at Fort Marion began to die at an alarming rate. The cramped conditions made it easier for disease to spread. There was little for the people to do, especially the men. Even the fort's commander pointed out that it was unhealthy to keep these formerly active Apache in indefinite idleness.

The government's education policy made things worse. More than 100 school-age Apache children were forcibly separated from their parents and sent to the infamous Indian School at Carlisle. What was called assimilation in the 1880s would now be viewed as an attempt at cultural genocide. The children were taken against their wishes, shipped to Pennsylvania, forced to cut their hair (an act of mourning in Native cultures), and given made-up names and "American" clothing to wear. The school forbade the children to speak their own language. Even worse, tuberculosis spread through Carlisle like wildfire, killing Native American children right and left.

Somehow, the Chiricahua at Fort Marion managed to maintain their equilibrium. From earliest childhood, the Chiricahua had been trained to accept hardships and disappointments. Nana reminded them that no matter how much they suffered, they were still Apache and must never complain. There was no disturbance or disobedience during their confinement. In their empty time, the Apache produced beadwork, bows, and arrows for sale in St. Augustine. The prisoners became a tourist attraction and some sympathetic local Floridians tried to help them.

With the Apache wars over, some Americans began to inquire into the treatment of the Apache prisoners of war. American public opinion was outraged when the press revealed that peaceable Apache were living in subhuman conditions at Fort Marion while some of their family members were being held at Fort Pickens against the terms of the surrender agreement. The uproar allowed Geronimo and the other men to join their families at Fort Marion in April 1887. However, there would be no return to the Southwest, even in the distant future. The Chiricahua had escaped with nothing more than their lives.

MOUNT VERNON BARRACKS, ALABAMA

In May 1888, the Chiricahua were congregated at the 2,000-acre (809.3-ha) Mount Vernon barracks in Alabama. "We were not healthy in this place," Geronimo said, "for the climate disagreed with us." The soil was unsuited for agriculture and the work was simply prison camp labor. An alarming number of Chiricahua died from malaria and tuberculosis. The one positive note was that, except for the young people at the Indian School in Carlisle, the Chiricahua were finally together again.

The next six years were particularly bleak. The post doctor was Walter Reed, who would later gain great fame for his fight against yellow fever. Yet even he was powerless to reduce the death rate. Of the Apache sent to Florida in 1886, 120 had died (almost 25 percent) by 1890, including 30 children who died at the Carlisle school.

The Apache prisoners tried to have a normal life at the Mount Vernon barracks. They told the old stories around the campfires, trained tribal dancers, and celebrated weddings and ceremonials. Eighty-one babies were born. All their supervisors reported on their good conduct, their cheerfulness, and their industry. An on-site school opened in 1889, and the always-practical Geronimo became an enthusiastic supporter. He recognized that the Apache would need "American" learning in the future, if there were a future. Still, there was not much to do. Many Chiricahua played cards and gambled. Some converted to Christianity. Almost all suffered from sickness, depression, the unhealthy moist atmosphere, and "the dreary monotony of empty lives."

In 1890, George Crook, now a major general, visited the prison camp. In his report, Crook wrote that by the "most ordinary justice" those American Indians who had served the government should not be held as prisoners. "Their farms have been taken from them, and others should be given to them. I cannot too strongly urge that immediate steps be taken to secure a reservation for them" where they could "work for themselves" and receive the "full benefit of their labors."

Crook tried to advocate for the Chiricahua in Florida but politics was never his strong suit. His last contribution recommended moving the Apache to Fort Sill in Oklahoma (then Indian Territory). He died of a heart attack two months later.

All his life, Crook had tried to do the right thing. He had lived by a code of honor and attempted to act with compassion and keep his word. Yet his most lasting work was to destroy the Apache culture that he so admired.

The Apache had a mixed view of General Crook. One warrior said, "Crook was our enemy; but though we hated him, we respected him and even [Geronimo] thought he would keep his promise. I think that he was honest in his promise but that he was not permitted to keep it." Geronimo never forgave him, however. "I think that General Crook's death," said Geronimo, "was sent by the Almighty as a punishment for the many evil deeds he committed."

FORT SILL, OKLAHOMA

The War Department still did not know what to do with Geronimo and the Chiricahua prisoners. Indian Territory had ceased to exist in 1890 when Oklahoma was opened to white settlement. The people of New Mexico and especially Arizona were hostile to the return of any Apache. Yet the young people who attended the Carlisle Indian School rarely assimilated into white society. Instead, as soon as they were able, they returned to join their families who were still prisoners.

In fall of 1894, the U.S. government moved the Chiricahua prisoners of war to Fort Sill, Oklahoma. The Kiowa and Comanche who lived there had never been friends of the Apache but they had the typical Native American sympathy for a homeless people. They consented to the relocation of the Apache as long as they remained on the military reservation. The Apache were thrilled to leave Alabama. Unfortunately, Geronimo's teenage son Chappo died from tuberculosis just before the move was completed.

Conditions were much better at Fort Sill than in Alabama or Florida. The men learned cattle ranching and planted sorghum and hay. They raised more than 250,000 melons and cantaloupes the first year. Geronimo even overcame his contempt for agriculture and farmed a little. The prisoners settled into a somewhat decent life. They lived with other Native peoples, walked on clean grass, and breathed pure western air. They saw mountains, even if they were not the rugged mountains of their Southwestern homeland.

Geronimo would live out the remaining 15 years of his life as a prisoner of war at Fort Sill. The soldiers called him "Gerry," a nickname that the once-feared warrior hated. He enjoyed horseracing, gambling, and drinking. Not surprisingly, he remained a prickly character until the end. All his life he had been a warrior; now there was no legitimate outlet for his energy. Captain Hugh Scott, a good friend of the Apache, found Geronimo "an unlovely character, a cross-grained, mean, selfish old curmudgeon, of whom . . . I never heard recounted a kindly or generous deed."

In 1894, Geronimo and his family settled in Fort Sill, Oklahoma, along with 341 other Chiricahua Apache. They had been promised the lands surrounding the fort, but local settlers resisted their settlement.

Nonetheless, others who knew Geronimo talked about his kindly spirit. E.A. Burbank, who painted Geronimo's portrait, struck up a sort of friendship with him. Burbank said he found it hard to visualize Geronimo "as the leader of a band of ravaging savages. To me he was a kind old man."

The years passed and the Chiricahua were still prisoners of war who yearned to go home. No other tribe suffered such punishment for their resistance. Tuberculosis continued to ravage the tribe. "We are vanishing from the Earth," said Geronimo, "yet I cannot think we are useless or Ussen would not have created us.... How long will it be until it is said, there are no Apaches?"

PUBLIC CELEBRITY

Over time, Geronimo began to meet more white civilians and developed a fierce business sense. He would sign autographs and sell pictures, and bows and arrows, but only for what he considered a proper amount of money. In many cases, he marked up souvenirs that others had made and sold them as his. Some people complained that the price was too high, but others noted that, after all, there was only one Geronimo.

With the end of the Indian Wars, Geronimo filled a nostalgic role for many Americans. He attended many national expositions and Wild West shows, often as the featured attraction. At the Pan-American Exposition at Buffalo in 1901, he received $45 per month and permission to select the group of Apache to accompany him. The old warrior was there when an assassin shot President William McKinley in September.

Geronimo was also one of the featured attractions of the St. Louis World's Fair of 1904. He rode a Ferris wheel, watched a puppet show, stared in amazement at the antics of a trained polar bear, and tried to figure out magic acts. As always, he sold souvenirs, making more money "than I have ever owned before." He appeared self-possessed, alert, and friendly to the crowds of people who came to see him. S. McGowan, who supervised Geronimo at the fair, admitted that, "He really has endeared himself to whites and Indians alike.... He was gentle, kind, and courteous. I did not think I could ever speak so kindly of the old fellow whom I have always regarded as an incarnate fiend." At the same time, he used every opportunity to plead for a return to his homeland.

In 1905, Stephen Barrett, superintendent of schools in nearby Lawton, Oklahoma, wanted to let Geronimo dictate his side of the story for publication. The U.S. Army officer in charge absolutely refused, and Barrett had to appeal directly to President Theodore

Roosevelt. After a long exchange of communications, the permission was finally granted.

Barrett then hired Asa Daklugie, Geronimo's nephew (actually he was his second cousin, the son of Juh), as a translator. Daklugie had been educated at Carlisle but was completely loyal to Apache traditions and history. The three men worked together on the book, the first account of the Apache wars from the Native side. As a factual account, the book suffers from Geronimo's fading memory. He was about 80 years old at the time and sometimes confused chronology and events. Still, the book's spirit is unmistakably Apache. Geronimo knew exactly what he wanted to say and was careful about which events he chose to portray. He refused to answer questions or change his narrative. It remains the best source for a view into Geronimo's character.

Geronimo was to have two more interactions with President Roosevelt. He rode a horse in Roosevelt's inauguration parade in Washington, D.C. Thousands of onlookers cheered for the old warrior on horseback. A few days later, he had a personal interview with the president. Geronimo took the opportunity to beg for the return of the Chiricahua to the Southwest. "Please, please take the rope from the hands of me and my people and let us be free," he pleaded. "We are tired of living in a strange land and want to go back to our old home. We will be good." Roosevelt refused his request, saying that the people of Arizona still hated Geronimo, and there would be trouble. Roosevelt concluded, "That is all I can say, Geronimo, except that I am sorry, and have no feeling against you."

GERONIMO AND RELIGION

The great labor of Geronimo's last 23 years was to try to understand what had happened to him and his people. All his life he had tried to do right, but now he and his people were prisoners of war with no sign of ever escaping. His personal life was little better. Two of Geronimo's wives had died in captivity and so did his three children—Chappo in Alabama and Fento and Lulu at Fort Sill. Even Geronimo's grandson died in 1908 at the age of 18. Of his many children, only Robert and Eva would survive him, and Eva only by two years.

All his life, he had been curious about the way the world worked. Now he wondered, why did everyone in his family seem to die and yet he lived on and on? His Power had promised him that no bullet would ever kill him and that he would live to be an old man. In 1858, this had seemed like a great gift, but now it appeared to be a joke of Ussen. Time after time, Geronimo told Daklugie that he wished he had stayed in Mexico and, like Victorio, fought until the last Apache died. It seemed that he had missed a warrior's death and instead had to watch the entire Chiricahua people die.

As a child, Geronimo learned to pray to Ussen. However, he said, the Apache "never prayed against any other person ... we ourselves took vengeance. We were taught that Ussen does not care for the petty quarrels of men." Asa Daklugie said, "We make no pretense of loving our enemies.... Have you ever known anybody who really did that? I have not. Ussen did not command that of the Apaches."

Now that he was in his eighties, Geronimo began to think about life after death. "The teachings of our tribe were not specific," he said. "We believed that there is a life after this one, but no one ever told me as to what part of man lived after death.... We hoped that in the future life family and tribal relations would be resumed."

Geronimo wondered, if the white man had won in the end, perhaps the white man's god was stronger than Ussen? The Dutch Reformed Church carried out the Christian missionary work among the Fort Sill Apache. In the late 1890s, Geronimo told the missionaries, "I, Geronimo, and these others are now too old to travel your Jesus road. But our children are young and I and my brothers will be glad to have the children taught about the white man's God." Some Apache did convert to Christianity, such as Naiche, Chihuahua, and Chatto.

Geronimo became a celebrity, appeared at several world fairs, traveled with Pawnee Bill's Wild West show, and even participated in President Theodore Roosevelt's inaugural parade. Still, he died as a prisoner of the United States at about age 85, regretting his decision to surrender.

In 1903, Geronimo was baptized in the Dutch Reformed Church. He said, "Since my life as a prisoner has begun I have heard the teachings of the white man's religion, and in many respects believe it to be better than the religion of my fathers. . . . Believing that in a wise way it is good to go to church, and that associating with Christians would improve my character, I have adopted the Christian religion."

Geronimo may have just been currying favor with whites; however, there is evidence that he was undergoing a sort of spiritual crisis. He was old and his Power seemed to have failed him to a degree. After his conversion, Geronimo stopped gambling, horseracing, and drinking for a time. However, in 1907, the church expelled Geronimo for gambling. To the end of his life, he seemed unsure of where he stood. He told Christian missionaries in 1908 that he wanted to start over while at the same time telling other Chiricahua that he held to the old Apache religion. It seems that he did not discard his traditional faith as much as supplement it with an overlay of some Christian beliefs.

TO THE HAPPY PLACE

In his autobiography, Geronimo expressed his desire to be "buried among those mountains" of the Southwest. "If this could be I might die in peace," he said, "feeling that my people, placed in their native homes, would increase in numbers, rather than diminish as at present, and that our name would not become extinct. . . . Could I but see this accomplished, I think I could forget all the wrongs that I have ever received, and die a contented and happy old man."

But it was not to be. He would never return to the Southwest, even for a brief visit. On a cold night in February 1909, Geronimo drank too much whiskey and fell from his horse. He lay on the ground in a ditch through the rest of the winter night. As a result, he contracted pneumonia and died at the post hospital on February 17. He was about 85 years old and had been a prisoner of war for 23 years.

Geronimo's Skull

Geronimo was buried at the Apache Indian Prisoner of War Cemetery at Fort Sill, Oklahoma. There, his body remains, alongside some of the most famous Apache leaders: Nana, Loco, Chihuahua, and the sons and grandsons of Cochise, Naiche, Juh, Mangas Coloradas, and Victorio.

Whether his body has rested peacefully is a different story. According to legend, three members of a powerful Yale secret society called the Skull and Bones stole Geronimo's skull and other remains in a grave robbery in 1918. To make the story more interesting, one of those three members was Prescott Bush, father of the forty-first president of the United States, George H.W. Bush, and grandfather of former president George W. Bush.

For many years, no one took the story seriously. Then, in 2005, a Yale University historian uncovered a 1918 letter by a Skull and Bones member that said, "The skull of the worthy Geronimo the Terrible, exhumed from its tomb at Fort Sill by your club … is now safe inside the (Tomb) together with his well worn femurs, bit & saddle horn."

In 2009, Geronimo's descendants sued Skull and Bones, claiming that its members stole Geronimo's remains. Geronimo's descendants say that they want to uncover any information that people know but have been keeping to themselves. Even if the bones at Yale are not those of Geronimo, they may still belong to one of the Apache prisoners who died at Fort Sill and should be returned.

Asa Daklugie remembered his uncle's death: "We could not burn his house; and, though he had not died in it, that should have been done out of respect. We could not bury his best war horse with him, but I saw that he had it for the journey. We placed his most treasured possessions in his grave. . . . He walks through eternity-garbed as a chief in his ceremonial robes and his medicine hat. He rides a fine horse. He has his best weapons."

9

HEALING OLD WOUNDS

"If I must die in bondage, I hope that the remnant of the Apache tribe may, when I am gone, be granted the one privilege which they request—to return to Arizona." This was the last sentence of Geronimo's autobiography, a desperate plea to return to the Southwest. Nor was he the only one to feel that way. In 1911, Naiche said, "All we want is to be freed and be released as prisoners and given land and homes that we can call our own. This is all we think about," said the chief. "Half or more than half of these people talk English. Half or more than half can read and write; they all know how to work. You have held us long enough. We want something else now."

Ironically, Geronimo helped achieve by his death what he could not do while he was living. His very name had always struck terror into Arizonans, and the Chiricahua Apache had been punished for 25 years. After he died, however, his enemies decided they did not have to hold Geronimo's people any longer in Oklahoma.

A law passed by the U.S. Congress in 1912 released the Chiricahua and allotted money for their settlement on land selected by the government. Arizona was out of the question because the white residents still hated the Chiricahua. Instead, the U.S. government decided that the best place would be the Mescalero Apache reservation in the newly admitted state of New Mexico.

The Mescalero Apache were the eastern neighbors of the Chiricahua. They were the Apache group closest to the Chiricahua in language and culture. These two tribes were normally at peace, had a reasonable amount of contact, and often helped each other during the troubled times in the late 1800s. The generous Mescalero were willing to accept the Chiricahua on equal terms and share the reservation.

Some of the Chiricahua prisoners wanted to remain in Oklahoma where they had lived for 27 years. These people were allowed to purchase individual farms from the heirs of deceased Comanche and Kiowa allottees. The U.S. government gave the 261 surviving Chiricahua the choice of remaining in Oklahoma or joining the Mescalero Apache reservation in New Mexico. The Chiricahua held many councils to help determine individual decisions.

Four years after Geronimo's death, the Chiricahua returned to their homeland; 183 chose to go to Mescalero while 78 decided to remain in Oklahoma. They arrived in New Mexico on April 4, 1913. It was not exactly home in Arizona, but it was close enough. One Chiricahua noted there were "Mountains in which to pray, wood, water, grass, abundance of game—and no White Eyes [whites]! Best of all, we could live among our own people and worship Ussen according to our own religion."

The Chiricahua who stayed in Oklahoma took up farms in rich agricultural land around the appropriately named town of Apache. In a way, they had to adjust to a more difficult life than the people of the reservation. The Oklahoma Chiricahua had to support themselves by farming and trades, and establish social relationships in a mostly white society. They were more likely to assimilate into mainstream American society than the Apache on the reservation. However, many of the Oklahoma Chiricahua have retained their strong sense of tribal identity. The Oklahoma and Mescalero bands have tried their best to maintain their contacts through frequent visits.

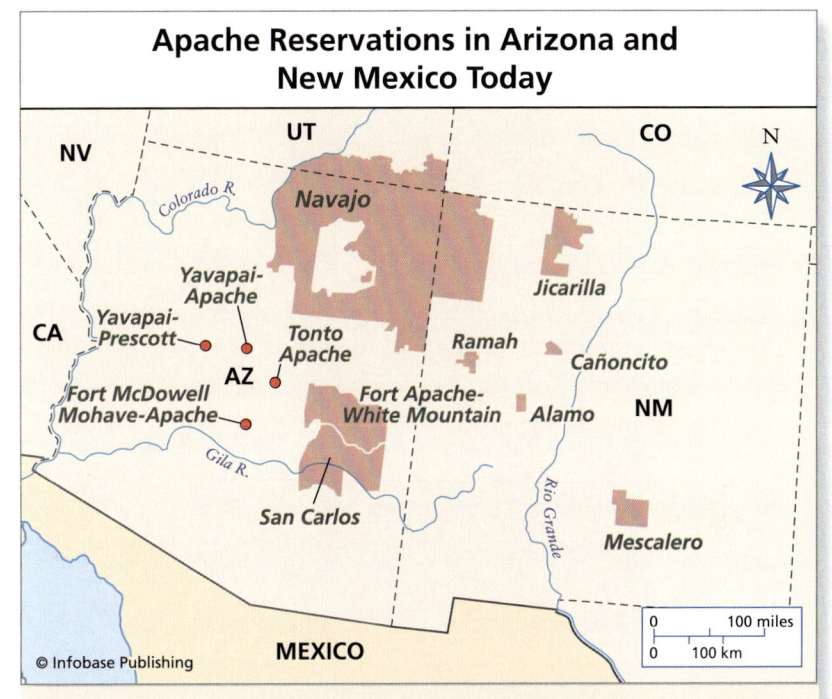

Apache Reservations in Arizona and New Mexico Today

Today, Apache live all over the country, from large urban areas to reservations in Arizona and New Mexico. This map shows the present-day locations of Apache peoples that live on reservations.

THE APACHE TODAY

The descendants of Geronimo, Naiche, Mangas, Victorio, and Nana mostly live today in Oklahoma or New Mexico. Like the members of all ethnic groups, they range in character from the virtuous to the unscrupulous, with most members falling somewhere in between. No one is alive anymore who can personally remember the raids, the hunted existence, and the bloody encounters with the armies of two nations.

Geronimo's bloodline did not die out. Of all his children, only Robert survived, but he lived until 1966 and had four sons. As of 2009, there were enough great-grandchildren left to be bitterly arguing with each other whether Geronimo's body should remain in Oklahoma or returned to New Mexico.

According to the 2000 census, the Apache population of the United States was 57,060. This placed them seventh among the largest Native American tribal groupings. Most of the Apache live on reservations totaling over 3 million acres (1.2 million hectares) in Arizona and New Mexico.

The Chiricahua population has increased since the U.S. government released them from captivity. They probably numbered about 1,200 in Cochise's prime; there were only about 500 left when the U.S. government shipped them to Florida as prisoners of war. By 1913, only 261 Chiricahua remained alive. As of 2000, however, the Chiricahua had rebounded to total 1,134. As a source of comparison, the same census lists the Jicarilla with 3,152; the Lipan, 131; and the Mescalero, 5,374.

Two large Apache reservations remain in Arizona today: the 1.67 million-acre (67.5 million hectare) White Mountain Apache Reservation (Fort Apache) and the 1.8 million-acre (728,000 hectare) San Carlos Apache Reservation in southeastern Arizona. The Fort Apache Reservation has the third-highest population of all Native American reservations in the United States.

A century has improved San Carlos slightly. San Carlos Lake, formed by the construction of Coolidge Dam in 1928, is Arizona's largest body of water. The lake serves as the center of the reservation's recreational activities. A gambling casino and a cultural center are also on the reservation. In 2000, the population of the San Carlos Apache was 9,716 but almost none of the Chiricahua live there.

Instead, the Mescalero and Chiricahua (and the Lipan) still share the 720-square-mile (1,864-sq-km) reservation in the mountains of southeast New Mexico. The Apache have tried to make the reservation self-supporting. Tourism is an important industry and the Ski Apache ski resort and hotel/casino is a major employer. Forest covers the majority of the land and timber harvesting provides some income. Summers are short, winters are cold, and there is very little tillable land so it remains unlikely that the Chiricahua there will ever become farmers. It is, however, excellent land for raising cattle. A more controversial source of income is a nuclear-waste

The Apache have fought to maintain their many tribal customs and traditions. The total Apache population today is about 60,000. There are 13 different Apache tribes, with their own government, laws, police, and services, and the largest reservation is the San Carlos Reservation.

storage site, approved by the Mescalero Apache after huge debate in the 1990s.

Many people think Native Americans somehow disappeared from American history after 1900. This is far from the case. The 2000 census showed that the United States population was 281 million; of that number 4.1 million, or 1.5 percent, reported they were of American Indian or Alaskan Native ancestry.

The Apache are no longer aggressive nomads who roam across the four-state area of Apachería. Instead, like most modern-day Americans, the Apache struggle to perform the careful balancing act of preserving the best parts of their traditional culture while facing the challenges of the twenty-first century.

THE IRONIES OF HISTORY

To the white settlers of Arizona and New Mexico, Geronimo was a merciless and savage murderer. This image of the Chiricahua leader endured until the second half of the 1900s. Now, Geronimo is frequently portrayed as a man who valiantly defended his people against the invasion of the United States into Apache tribal lands.

History can sometimes be extremely ironic. This means that there is a huge difference between the result that is expected and the result that actually occurs. Ironies abound in the story of Geronimo. For example, "facts" state that the United States won the Apache wars and the Apache lost them. Yet Major Generals George Crook and Nelson Miles are barely remembered; their supposedly brilliant military skill that would live long in history is completely forgotten. Only historians are able to say more than a few words about the presidents of the time—men such as Chester Arthur, Benjamin Harrison, and Grover Cleveland.

Yet the leaders of the Native tribes they ground into dust—Geronimo, Sitting Bull, Crazy Horse—remain alive in American culture. Almost every American recognizes the names of these great chiefs when the names of presidents and the generals are forgotten.

The greater irony is the way in which these American Indian leaders and their peoples are viewed. They are no longer the "skulking red devils" of popular nineteenth-century imagery. In 1880, General John Pope called the Apache "a miserable, brutal race, cruel, deceitful, and wholly irreclaimable." Samuel Cozzens described them as "sneaking, cowardly, and revengeful. They are always ready to assassinate women and children." Geronimo seemed to white Americans to be the very personification of these traits, a ruthless killer bent only on torture.

How these nineteenth-century Americans would be shocked to hear the Apache praised in the Congress of the United States. That the praise would come from a Southwestern representative would seem even stranger. Yet here was Harry Teague, New Mexico's representative in the U.S. House of Representatives, addressing Congress in support of U.S. Resolution 132:

Mr. Speaker, I rise today to commemorate the 100th year after the passing of Goyathlay.... Goyathlay's actions on behalf of his people have been commemorated in legends, history, and film. His skill and indomitable spirit live on as a memorial to the Apache people and their culture. Goyathlay fought to preserve the Apache from what he saw to be an invading force, one that was foreign to him and did not understand his people's ways and beliefs.... The values that they cherish, values that Goyathlay fought so hard to preserve, are still alive in them today.

On the anniversary of Goyathlay's death, we hope that we as a people and Nation have moved beyond the differences that separated us 100 years ago. We hope that we can begin a process to heal old wounds and ensure that everyone's voices are heard, their needs are met.

CHRONOLOGY

c. 1500   Apache enter the Southwest.

c. 1600   Spanish enter the Southwest.

1821   Mexico wins independence from Spain.

c. 1825   Apache Goyathlay ("One Who Yawns"), later known as Geronimo, is born in present-day New Mexico.

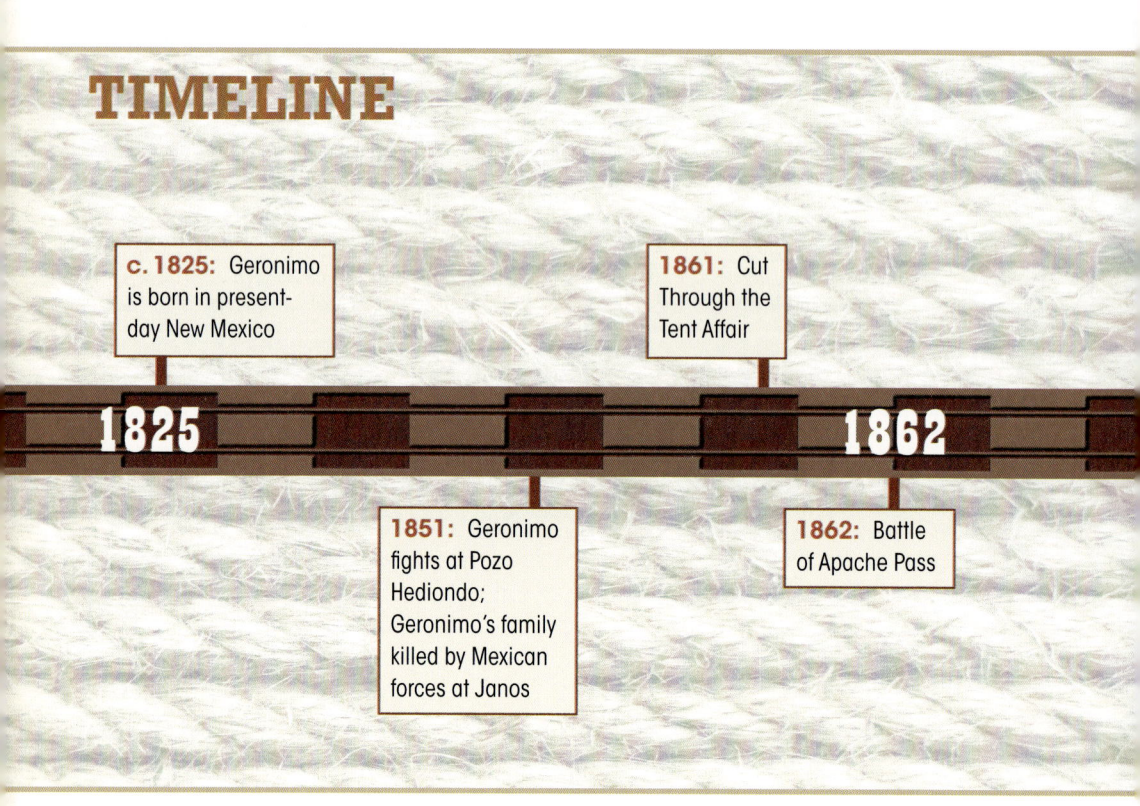

TIMELINE

c. 1825: Geronimo is born in present-day New Mexico

1851: Geronimo fights at Pozo Hediondo; Geronimo's family killed by Mexican forces at Janos

1861: Cut Through the Tent Affair

1862: Battle of Apache Pass

1825 — **1862**

1848 Mexican-American War ends.

1849 California Gold Rush begins.

1854 The United States gains control of a 29,000-square-mile region of present-day southern Arizona and southwestern New Mexico in a treaty called the Gadsden Purchase. The purpose is to construct a railroad along a deep southern route. This purchase includes the heart of Chiricahua Apache territory.

1861–1865 Eleven Southern states break away from the United States and form the Confederate States of America. This leads to the American Civil War and the end of slavery in the United States.

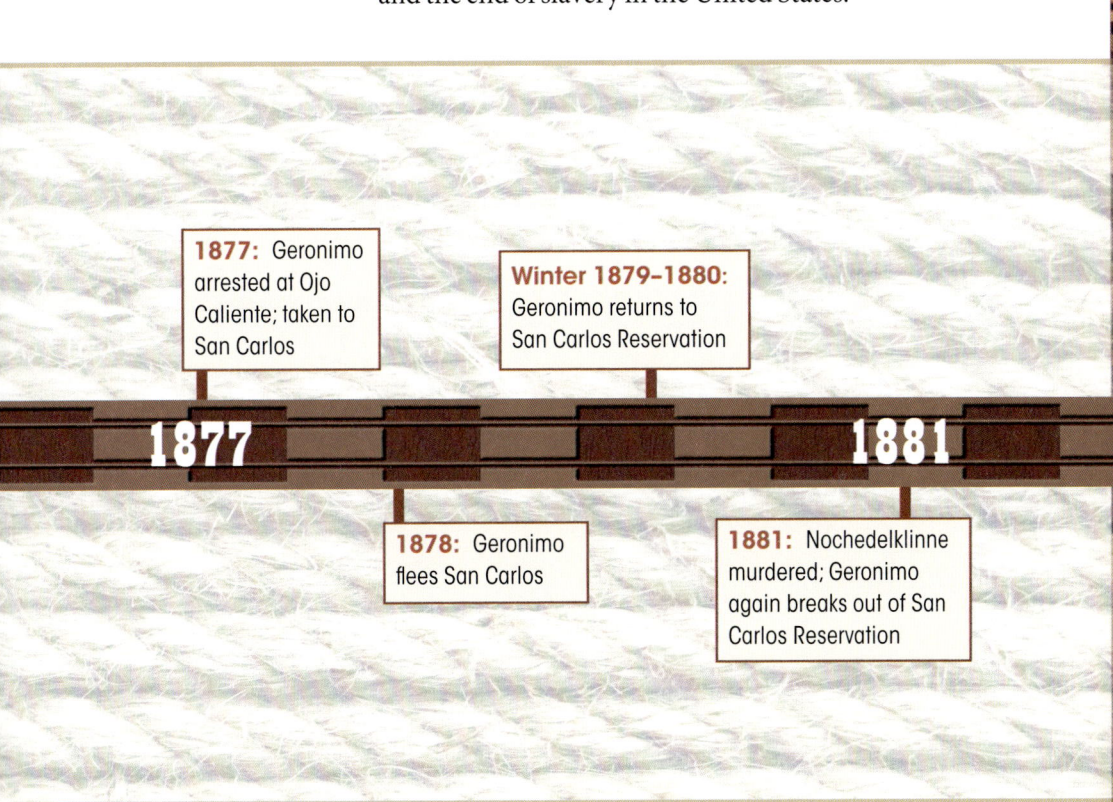

1877: Geronimo arrested at Ojo Caliente; taken to San Carlos

Winter 1879–1880: Geronimo returns to San Carlos Reservation

1877

1881

1878: Geronimo flees San Carlos

1881: Nochedelklinne murdered; Geronimo again breaks out of San Carlos Reservation

1861 A series of conflicts fought between American settlers and Apache tribes, called Apache wars, begins.

1863 Apache chief Mangas Coloradas ("Red Sleeves"), thought to be one of the most important Native American leaders of the nineteenth century, is murdered by U.S. soldiers, allegedly trying to escape custody. U.S. soldiers cut off his head and send the skull to the Smithsonian.

1871 American settlers, Mexicans, and O'odham attack Apache, mostly women and children, while the Apache men are off hunting in the mountains. One-hundred forty-four Aravaipas and Pinals are murdered. This becomes known as the Camp Grant massacre.

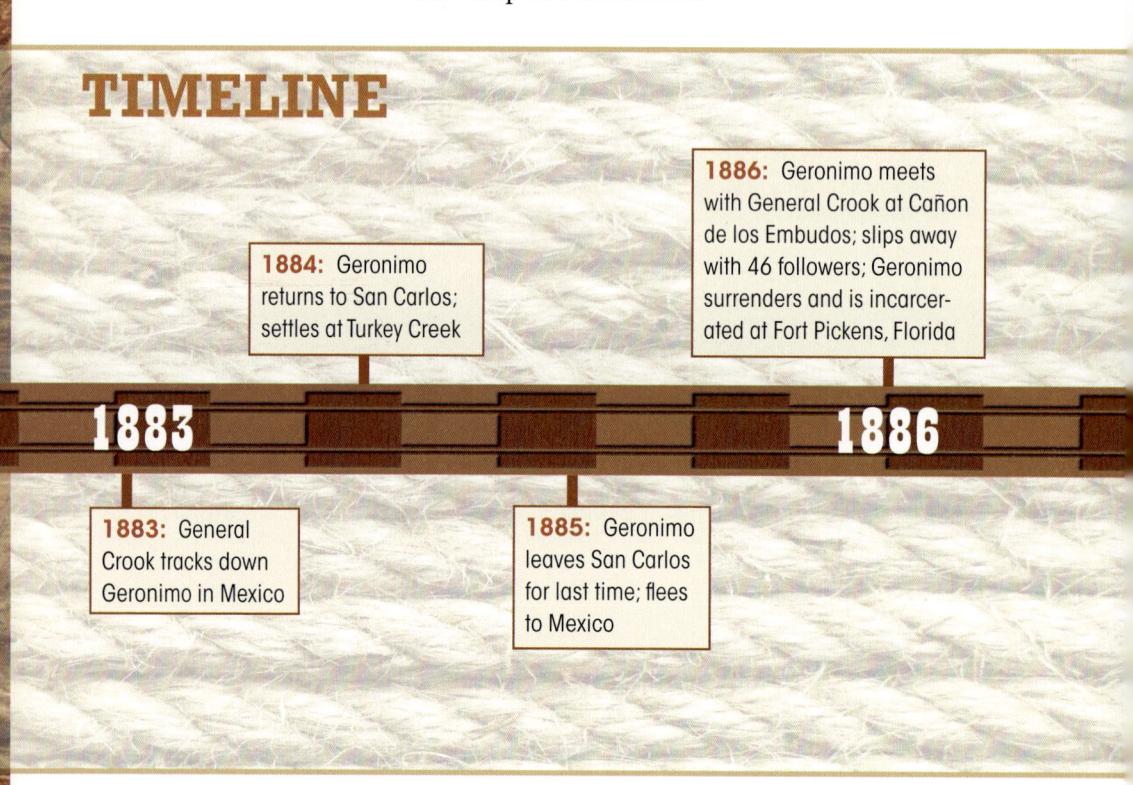

TIMELINE

1884: Geronimo returns to San Carlos; settles at Turkey Creek

1886: Geronimo meets with General Crook at Cañon de los Embudos; slips away with 46 followers; Geronimo surrenders and is incarcerated at Fort Pickens, Florida

1883

1886

1883: General Crook tracks down Geronimo in Mexico

1885: Geronimo leaves San Carlos for last time; flees to Mexico

1872 Chief Cochise makes treaty with U.S. creating a separate Chiricahua reservation.

1874 Cochise dies on an Arizona reservation of natural causes.

1875 The Department of the Interior decides to consolidate all Apache at San Carlos.

1876 The San Carlos reservation is revoked after the Chiricahua flee south, deeper into Mexico or to the Ojo Caliente Reservation.

1880 Chief Victorio, previously successful at evading capture by U.S. military, is ambushed at Tres Castillos and killed by Mexican soldiers.

1881 Chiricahua leader and Geronimo's brother-in-law, Kas-tziden, also known as Nana, leads

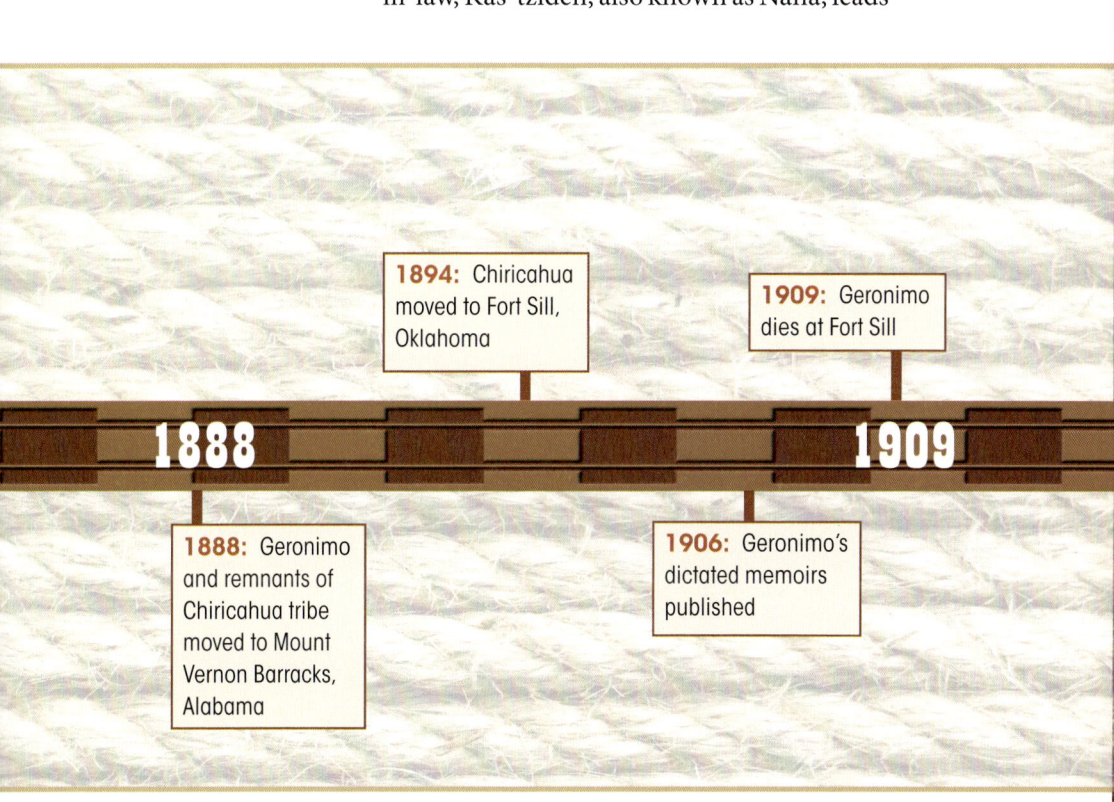

1888 — **1909**

1894: Chiricahua moved to Fort Sill, Oklahoma

1909: Geronimo dies at Fort Sill

1888: Geronimo and remnants of Chiricahua tribe moved to Mount Vernon Barracks, Alabama

1906: Geronimo's dictated memoirs published

several raids on U.S. Army supply trains and American settlers. He is captured in a surprise attack and sent to San Carlos but escapes and joins forces with Geronimo in Mexico.

1886 Able to elude capture in the past, Geronimo finally surrenders to General Miles at Skeleton Canyon, Arizona.

1901–1905 In his old age, Geronimo becomes a celebrity, starring as the main attraction at world fairs and selling souvenirs and photographs of himself. He rides in President Theodore Roosevelt's inauguration parade in Washington, D.C., and has his life story written in a book.

1909 Geronimo dies of pneumonia as a prisoner of the United States at Fort Sill, Oklahoma.

1913 Most Chiricahua return to Mescalero Reservation in New Mexico.

1940 Soldiers from 501st Parachute Infantry Regiment first yell "Geronimo."

2000 Census shows 57,000 Apache and 1,134 Chiricahua.

2009 U.S. House of Representatives pass Resolution 132, which honors the life of Geronimo and recognizes the one-hundredth anniversary of his death.

Geronimo's descendants sue Yale's Skull and Bones secret society for alleged theft of Geronimo's skull.

GLOSSARY

Apache Pass Pass in Arizona between the Dos Cabezas and Chiricahua Mountains. It was the site of Apache Spring, an important water source. Several incidents took place there between the Apache and Union Army soldiers.

Apachería Term for the traditional area inhabited by the Apache. The region covered several thousand square miles, mainly in Arizona, New Mexico, and the northern states of Mexico.

Apache scouts Apache who served as paid U.S. Army Indian scouts. They were widely and effectively used by General George Crook in the Apache wars in the late 1800s.

assimilation The blending of minority groups into the dominant society. White Americans in the 1800s offered the Apache the choice of assimilation or extermination.

Bedonkohe One of the bands of the Chiricahua Apache. Geronimo was a member of this band.

Buffalo Soldiers Native American nickname for several African-American cavalry units who fought in the American west in the late 1800s. They participated in several battles against the Apache.

Chiricahua One of the main regional branches of the Apache. Geronimo, Cochise, and Mangas Coloradas were members of this group.

company Military unit of approximately 50 to 200 soldiers. Most companies consist of two to five platoons.

Congressional Resolution Official statement of position by one or both houses of the U.S. Congress. It carries no legal authority but reflects the nation's current opinion on a particular subject as interpreted by the peoples' elected representatives.

Gadsden Purchase In 1854, the United States paid $10 million to Mexico for a small strip of land (29,000 square miles) across southern Arizona and New Mexico. This purchase included the heart of Chiricahua Apache territory.

Ghost Dance Religious dance of Native Americans hoping for communication with the dead and the coming of an American Indian messiah who would make the whites disappear and restore the land to the American Indians. In 1881, an Apache mystic named Nochedelklinne introduced the Ghost Dance to the Apache with tragic results.

malaria Disease that involves high fevers, shaking chills, and flu like symptoms. It is caused by a parasite spread by the bite of infected *Anopheles* mosquitoes. The Apache suffered many malaria-related deaths when they were moved to Florida.

rations Portion assigned to a person or group. By treaty, the Apache were often entitled to food, clothing, and other rations in exchange for their cooperation or the "sale" of their land.

reservation Area that is reserved for a specific purpose. In the 1800s, the U.S. government set aside specific areas reserved for Native Americans and tried to force most Native Americans to live there.

San Carlos Apache Reservation (about 28,957 square miles or 7,500 square kilometers) established in 1871 in southeastern Arizona. Geronimo lived there for several years.

shaman Person supposedly possessing supernatural powers to communicate between the visual and the spirit world. Native American shamans like Geronimo were the spiritual leaders of tribes. They could heal the sick and enter the supernatural world to receive answers to the problems of the community.

telegraph Electrical device for sending and receiving messages over long distances. It became popular in the United States in the 1840s. For most of the 1800s, it was the only way to convey information quickly over very long distances.

tizwin Fermented drink made from corn that was greatly loved by the Apache. It had a relatively low alcoholic counter and spoiled quickly so the Apache would make large batches and drink it quickly in vast quantities at feasts.

Treaty of Guadalupe Hidalgo Peace treaty that ended the Mexican-American War in 1848. It awarded more than one million square kilometers to the United States, including California, Arizona, and New Mexico, the traditional homelands of the Apache.

tribe Social group made up of many families, clans, or generations. Tribal members usually share values and organize themselves for mutual care and defense.

Tucson Ring Informal group of Arizona merchants and army contractors in the late 1800s. They profited from supplying the U.S. Army with food, forage, horses, and equipment and constantly lobbied and instigated against the Apache "threat."

Ussen Apache deity, usually considered a remote Supreme Being, sometimes called "Life Giver." There are a variety of spellings.

BIBLIOGRAPHY

Aleshire, Peter. *The Fox and the Whirlwind: General George Crook and Geronimo, A Paired Biography*. New York: John Wiley, 2000.

"American Indian and Alaska Native Population—2000," Census 2000 Brief. Available online. URL: http://www.census.gov/prod/2002pubs/c2kbr01-15.pdf

Andrist, Ralph K. *The Long Death: The Last Days of the Plains Indians*. Norman: University of Oklahoma Press, 1964.

Annerino, John. *Apache: The Sacred Path to Womanhood*. Emeryville, Calif.: Marlowe and Company, 1998.

"Apache," Funk and Wagnalls New Encyclopedia–2006. Available online. URL: http://www.history.com/encyclopedia.do?vendorId=FWNE.fw..ap119900.a#FWNE.fw..ap119900.a.

Ball, Eve. *In the Days of Victorio: Recollections of a Warm Springs Apache*. Tucson: University of Arizona Press, 1970.

Ball, Eve, with Nora Henn and Lynda A. Sanchez. *Indeh: An Apache Odyssey*. Norman: University of Oklahoma Press, 1980.

Barrett, S. M., ed. *Geronimo: His Own Story, The Autobiography of a Great Patriot Warrior*. New York: Ballantine Books, 1971 [1906].

Basso, Keith H. *Portraits of "the Whiteman": Linguistic Play and Cultural Symbols among the Western Apache*. Cambridge, UK: Cambridge University Press, 1979.

Basso, Keith H., and Morris E. Opler. *Apachean Culture, History, and Ethnology*. Tucson: University of Arizona Press, 1971.

Beal, Tom. "Curing 'Amnesia' about State's Most Blood-soaked Day," *Arizona Daily Star*, May 3, 2009.

Bibliography

Betzinez, Jason, and Wilbur Sturtevant Nye. *I Fought with Geronimo*. Harrisburg, PA: The Stackpole Company, 1959.

Bourke, John Gregory. *On the Border with Crook*. New York: Charles Scribner's Sons, 1891.

"Butterfield Overland Mail Record Book," National Postal Museum. Available online. URL: http://www.postalmuseum.si.edu/museum/1d_Butterfield.html.

Clum, Woodworth. *Apache Agent: The Story of John P. Clum*. Boston: Houghton Mifflin, 1936.

Colwell-Chanthaphonh, Chip. *Massacre at Camp Grant: Forgetting and Remembering Apache History*. Tucson: University of Arizona Press, 2007.

Crook, George. *General George Crook: His Autobiography*. Ed. Martin F. Schmitt. Norman: University of Oklahoma Press, 1946.

Daniels, Bruce. "Geronimo Family Feud Escalates," *Albuquerque Journal*, May 6, 2009. Available online. URL: http://www.abqjournal.com/abqnews/index.php?option=com_content&view=article&id=10846:635am-geronimo-died-100-years-ago-today&catid=1:latest&Itemid=39&y.

Davis, Britton. *The Truth about Geronimo*. New Haven: Yale University Press, 1929.

Debo, Angie. *Geronimo: The Man, His Time, His Place*. Norman: University of Oklahoma Press, 1976.

Faulk, Odie B. *The Geronimo Campaign*. New York: Oxford University Press, 1969.

Ferg, Alan, ed. *Western Apache Material Culture: The Goodwin and Guenther Collections*. Tucson: University of Arizona Press, 1987.

"Found Letter Says Yale Club Has Geronimo Skull," Associated Press, May 9, 2006. Available online. URL: http://www.msnbc.msn.com/id/12591414/.

Gardner, Mark L. *Geronimo: A Biography*. Tucson: Western National Parks Association, 2006.

"Geronimo's Kin Sue Skull and Bones," Associated Press, February 18, 2009. Available online. URL: http://www.msnbc.msn.com/id/29265600/.

Goodwin, Grenville, and Neil Goodwin. *The Apache Diaries: A Father-Son Journey.* Lincoln: University of Nebraska Press, 2000.

Haley, James L. *Apaches: A History and Culture Portrait.* Norman: University of Oklahoma Press, 1981.

Harden, Paul. "Nana's Raid—Apaches in Socorro County," *El Defensor Chieftain*, July 3, 2004. Available online. URL: http://www.dchieftain.com/news/42295-07-03-04.html.

"Honoring Apache Leader Goyathlay [Geronimo]," *Congressional Record*, February 23, 2009. Available online. URL: http://www.sancarlosapache.org/HOUSERES132.html.

"Inn of the Mountain Gods Resort and Casino." Available online. URL: http://www.innofthemountaingods.com/index.asp.

Jacoby, Karl. *Shadows at Dawn: A Borderlands Massacre and the Violence of History.* New York: Penguin Press, 2008.

Kraft, Louis. *Gatewood and Geronimo.* Albuquerque: University of New Mexico Press, 2000.

Leckie, William H. *The Buffalo Soldiers: A Narrative of the Negro Cavalry in the West.* Norman: University of Oklahoma Press, 1967.

McKanna, Clare V., Jr. *White Justice in Arizona: Apache Murder Trials in the Nineteenth Century.* Lubbock, TX: Texas Tech University Press, 2005.

Miles, Nelson. *Personal Recollections and Observations of General Nelson A. Miles.* Lincoln: University of Nebraska Press, 1992 [1896].

"Old Apache Chief Geronimo Is Dead." *New York Times*, February 18, 1909. Available online. URL: http://www.nytimes.com/learning/general/onthisday/bday/0616.html.

Opler, Morris E. *Apache Odyssey: A Journey between Two Worlds.* Lincoln: University of Nebraska Press, 2002 [1969].

Roberts, David. *Once They Moved Like the Wind: Cochise, Geronimo, and the Apache Wars.* New York: Simon and Schuster, 1993.

Silva, Lee A. "Warm Springs Apache Leader Nana: The 80-Year-Old Warrior Turned the Tables," *Wild West* (December 2006).

Available online. URL: http://www.historynet.com/warm-springs-apache-leader-nana-the-80-year-old-warrior-turned-the-tables.htm.

Simmons, Marc. "Trail Dust: Famed Warrior Geronimo Had Complex Life," *New Mexican*, March 3, 2009. Available online. URL: http://www.santafenewmexican.com/SantaFeNorthernNM/Famed-warrior-Geronimo-had-complex-life.

Sweeney, Edwin R. *Cochise: Chiricahua Apache Chief*. Norman: University of Oklahoma Press, 1991.

Thrapp, Dan L. *The Conquest of Apachería*. Norman: University of Oklahoma Press, 1967.

Watt, Eva Tulene, with Keith H. Basso. *Don't Let the Sun Step Over You: A White Mountain Apache Family Life, 1860–1975*. Tucson: University of Arizona Press, 2004.

FURTHER RESOURCES

Aleshire, Peter. *Warrior Woman: The Story of Lozen, Apache Warrior and Shaman*. New York: St. Martin's Press, 2001.

Brown, Dee. *Bury My Heart at Wounded Knee: An Indian History of the American West*. New York: Bantam, 1971.

Opler, Morris E. *An Apache Life-Way: The Economic, Social, and Religious Institutions of the Chiricahua Indians*. Chicago: University of Chicago Press, 1965.

Reedstrom, E. Lisle. *Apache Wars: An Illustrated Battle History*. New York: Sterling Publishing, 1990.

Robinson, Sherry. *Apache Voices: Their Stories of Survival as told to Eve Ball*. Albuquerque: University of New Mexico Press, 2000.

Sweeney, Edwin R. *Mangas Coloradas: Chief of the Chiricahua Apaches*. Norman: University of Oklahoma Press, 1998.

Thrapp, Dan L. *Victorio and the Mimbrés Apaches*. Norman: University of Oklahoma Press, 1974.

Web sites

American Indian Heritage Association

http://www.indians.org/welker/geronimo.htm

A comprehensive Web site established by the American Indian Heritage Association. There are biographies, photographs, a tribal directory, instructions on tracing Indian heritage, and the latest news. The site also features a Geronimo page.

Apache History along the Geronimo Trail, National Scenic Byway

http://www.geronimotrail.com/pdf/apache-booklet.pdf

This site is an online version of the booklet detailing the Geronimo Trail National Scenic Byway and a brief history of the Apache people in New Mexico. Black-and-white and color photographs are included.

Apache Indian Language Links

http://www.native-languages.org/apache.htm

This site is a resource for studying Apache language, history, and mythology.

Apache Nation Chamber of Commerce

http://www.sancarlosapache.com/home.htm

The official Web site of the Apache Nation Chamber of Commerce features information about attractions, businesses, news, and the tribal nations within Apache society.

Apache Nation Cultural & Historical Organization

http://www.chiricahuaapache.org/about_ANCHO.htm

Founded in 2000, this nonprofit organization supports various cultural and restoration projects for the unification of the Apache nation.

Arizona Apache Wars

http://www.geocities.com/~zybt/awars.htm

This site features a treatise on the Apache wars and analyzes how they affected Arizona.

Chiricahua Apache Nde Nation

http://www.chiricahuaapache.org/

This is the official site of the Chiricahua Apache Nde Nation. It includes a biography of Geronimo, a speaking dictionary, maps, Chiricahua quotations, and 7-Natural Laws of the tribe.

Fort Bowie National Historic Site

http://www.nps.gov/fobo/

Fort Bowie National Historic Site is protected by the U.S. Department of Interior's National Park Service. Fort Bowie allows visitors to tour several important sites, including the Butterfield Stage Station, the Post Cemetery, a replica of the Chiricahua Apache Camp, and Apache Spring.

Harry Hoijer's Chiricahua and Mescalero Apache Texts
http://etext.lib.virginia.edu/apache/
Available to the public for free, this text is part of the multilingual collection at the University of Virginia's Electronic Text Center at Alderman Library. The document contains a set of 55 Apache language texts, including songs, prayers, and speeches.

New Mexico Tourism Department—Geronimo Trail National Scenic Byway
http://www.newmexico.org/explore/scenic_byways/geronimo.php
Visitors' information on exhibits, beautiful landscapes, and western towns by way of a scenic highway tour through New Mexico.

PICTURE CREDITS

Page

- 8: © AP Images
- 11: © SSgt. Marlene S. Barry/DefenseImagery.mil
- 15: © Infobase Publishing
- 17: © Infobase Publishing
- 26: © Private Collection/The Bridgeman Art Library
- 31: © Peter Newark American Pictures/The Bridgeman Art Library
- 33: © Denver Public Library, Western History Collection
- 37: © Infobase Publishing
- 41: © Time Life Pictures/US Signal Corps/Time Life Pictures/Getty Images
- 47: Courtesy of the Library of Congress Prints & Photographs Division, LC-USZ62-52494
- 54: © Shutterstock
- 58: © Legends of America
- 63: © National Portrait Gallery, Smithsonian Institution/Art Resource, NY
- 67: Courtesy of the Library of Congress Prints & Photographs Division, LC-USZC2-6296
- 71: © Corbis
- 74: © Time Life Pictures/US Signal Corps/Time Life Pictures/Getty Images
- 78: © MPI/Getty Images
- 80: © Camillus S Fly/Getty Images
- 85: Courtesy of the Library of Congress Prints & Photographs Division, 23781r/LC-DIG-gg-bain-23781
- 89: © AP Images
- 94: © MPI/Getty Images
- 98: © Denver Public Library, Western History Collection, Ed Irwin, X-32893
- 103: © Infobase Publishing
- 105: © M.L Pearson/Alamy

123

INDEX

Page numbers in *italics* indicate photos or illustrations, and page numbers followed by *m* indicate maps.

A

African-Americans 58, 77–79
Alabama 91–92
alcoholism 62
Aliso Creek 67
Alope (wife) 14, 28, 34
ambushes 40–41
Apache, Fort 73, 103*m*, 104
Apache Pass 39–41, 48
Apache Pass, Battle of 40–41
Apache people. *See also Specific groups*
current 103–105, 103*m*, 105
family life of 32–34
fighting strategy of 21–24
language of 22–23
life of 18–20
overview of 15–16, 15*m*, 17
raiding by 20–21
Apache Wars 9, 43–46, 95–96

Apachería 15–16, 15*m*, 36
apprenticeships 18
Aravaipa Apache 44–45
Arizona 36–38, 37*m*, 49. *See also* Tucson
autobiography 95–96, 101
autographs 95

B

baptism 99
Barrett, Stephen 95
Bascom, George 39–40
Bascom Affair 40, 43
Baylor, John 42
beatings 75
Bedonkohe Apache 13, *17*, 43. *See also* Chiricahua Apache
Betzinez, Jason (cousin) 18, 29
birth of Geronimo 10
boasting 22
bounties 21
Bowie, Fort 41, *41*, 78, 87
Bowie Reservation 46–48
Buchanan, Fort 39, 40
Buffalo Soldiers 59, 77–79, 78

bullets 34–35
Burbank, E.A. 94
Bush, Prescott 100
Butterfield, John 38
Butterfield Overland Mail 38, 39

C

California 36–37, 38
California Volunteers 40–41
Camp Grant Massacre 44–46
Cañon de los Embudos 79–80, *80*
Carlisle Indian School 22, 90, 91
Carlton, James 42
Carr, Eugene 62
Carrasco, José María 27–28
cattle 73, 104
celebrity 95–96, *98*
cemetery 100
census data 104
Cerro Tres Castillos 59
Chappo (son) 32, 93, 97
Chatto 68, 69, 76, 90
Cheehashkish (wife) 32, 67
Chihenne Apache 43
Chihuahua (chief) 63, 68, 70

124

Index

Chihuahua, Mexico 25–28, 30
Chiricahua Apache 39–41, 52–53, 55, 104. See also Bedonkohe Apache
Chiricahua Reservation 51
Chokonen Apache 43
Cibecue Creek 62
Civil War 42, 43, 48, 61, 81
Cleveland, Grover 88
clothing 30–31
Clum, John 52–53, 56, 64, 70–71
Cochise 39–41, 43–44, 46–48, 50
Comanche 93, 102
commissioned officers 61
companies 61
Congressional Resolution 132 7, 10, 13, 27, 106–107
corn 20
counting coup 22–23
Cozzens, Samuel 106
Crawford, Emmet 72
Crazy Horse 12
Crook, George 22–23, 49–51, 57, 69–82, *80*, 92, 106
crops 19
Cushing, Howard 43
Cut Through the Tent Affair 40, 43

D

Daklugie, Asa (nephew) 96, 97, 100
Davis, Britton 72, 74
death of Geronimo 99–100

diseases 55, 90, 91, 93, 94
Dohnsay (daughter) 32
Dragoon Mountain 46, 48
Dutch Reformed Church 97

E

Earp brothers 64
education 14, 22, 90
enlisted officers 61
Eskiminzin 44
Eva (daughter) 97

F

family life 32–34
farming 73–75, *74*, 93, 102
Fento (son) 97
Florida 84–86, 87, 88–91, *89*
Fly, C.S. *80*, 80
Fort Bowie Reservation 46–48
forts 39

G

Gadsden Purchase 37–39, 37*m*
gambling 99
Gatewood, Charles 72, 84–86
Ghost Dance 62
Gold Rush 36–37
Goyathlay, as birth name 13
Grant, Camp 44–46
Grant, Ulysses S. 44, 46, 51
grave robbery 100
Guadalupe Hidalgo, Treaty of 36, 37*m*
guerrilla warfare 23

H

Happy Place 42, 99–100
Hart, Henry Lyman 53
horses 14, 21, 23, 27
Howard, Oliver Otis 46, *47*
howitzers 41
hunting 17–18, 19–20, 48

I

Ihtedda (wife) 34
interpretation, history and 9–10, 106–107
irrigation 73, *74*

J

Jeffords, Thomas 46, 50
Juana (mother) 13–14, 28
judge, killing of 69
Juh 43, 46, 51–52, 55, 65–66, 70

K

Kanseah 82–83
Kautz, August 51
Kayitah 84, 90
Kaytennae 76, 84
Kiowa Apache 16, 93, 102

L

languages 22–23
Lawton, Henry 83
Life Giver 14, 35, 97
Lipan Apache 104
Loco *63*, 66–68, 76
Lozen 83
Lulu (child) 97

M

Mahko (grandfather) 13
mail 38, 39, 56
Mangas Coloradas 25, 27, 41, 42–43
Marion, Fort 88–89, 90–91
Marlanetta (wife) 33
marriage 14
Martine 84, 90
McGowan, S. 95
McKinley, William 95
McLane, Fort 42
medicine men 34, 35
mescal 20
Mescalero Apache 42, 104
Mescalero Apache reservation 102, 103*m*
Mexicans
  fighting with 25–32, *26*
  hatred for 12
  raiding of 21
  scalping by 29
  Victorio and 59
migratory culture 20
Miles, Nelson 81–87, *85*, 106
military 59–62
missionaries 97
Mount Vernon barracks 91–92
mules 48

N

Naiche 52, 63, *63*, 66, *67*, 70, 76, 79, 81, 84
Nana 60, *63*, 76, 79, 91
Nana's Raid 60, 62–63
Nanathathtith (wife) 32
Navajo 15*m*, 16, *17*
Nednhi Apache 14, *17*, 43
New Mexico 36, 42, 56, 102
nickname 27
Nochedelklinne 62
nuclear waste, storage of 104–105

O

Ojo Caliente Reservation 52, 57–59
Oklahoma 93–94, 102
Ord, Edward 56
Ormsby, Waterman 38
Oury, William 45
Overland Mail 38, 39
Oxbow Route 38

P

Pan-American Exposition 95
Papago Indians 44–45
paratroopers 10, *11*
parleys 45
Pickens, Fort 88–89, *89*, 91
polygamy 32–34
Pope, John 106
Power *31*, 34–35, 97, 99
Pozo Hediondo 27
prophecies 62

R

raiding 20–21, 30–32, 59–60, 65–68, 79
rations 48, 52, 55
Reed, Walter 91
religion 92, 96–99
renegades 52–53
reservations 46–48, 51–52, 57–59, 102–104, 103*m*. See also San Carlos Apache Reservation
resistance, symbol of 10–12
Rhyolite Canyon *78*
Robert (son) 97, 103
Roosevelt, Theodore 95–96

S

Safford, Anson 46, 50
San Carlos Apache Reservation 51–59, *54*, 62, 65, 70–77, 103*m*, 104
San Carlos Lake 104
scalping 25, 29
schools 14, 22, 90, 91
Scott, Hugh 93
scouts 49, *71*, 72–73, 81, 90
shamans 34, 35
sheep ranch incident 65
Sheridan, Phil 79, 81
Shesha (wife) 34
Shtshashe (wife) 34
Sierra Emmedio 66–67
Sill, Fort 92, 93–94, *94*, 97, 100
Sioux 22
Sitting Bull 12
Skeleton Canyon 86
Ski Apache resort 104
Skull and Bones 100
slavery 21
Smithsonian Museum 42
soldiers 59–62, 77–79, *78*
Sonora 27, 30
souvenirs 95
Stanley, D.S. 89

stealth 21–24
strychnine 45
suffering 14
supernatural *31*, 34–35, 97, 99

T

Taklishim (father) 13–14
Taza 51, 63
Teague, Harry 106–107
teepees 19
telegraph lines 56, 78
Tiffany, Joseph 55–56, 62
tizwin 20, 55, 75, 76
Tonto Apache 45
torture 29
tourism 104
trackers 49
Tucson 44–46, 53, 56–57

Tucson Ring 56–57
Turkey Creek 73–74, *74*

U

Ulzana 79
Ussen 14, 35, 97

V

vengeance 30
Victorio 29, 43, 52–53, 57–59, *58*, 83

W

Warm Springs band 52–53, 57–59, 65–66, 84–85
Warm Springs Reservation 52, 57–59
warriors 18, 24
Western Apache 72
whiskey 42

White Mountain Apache *71*, 73, 103*m*, 104
Whitman, Royal 44
wickiups *19*, 19
Wilcox, Orlando 51
witches 34, 40
wives 32–34, 75. See also *Specific wives*
Woman Warrior 83
Woolsey, King 45
world fairs 95, *98*
World War II 10, *11*
Wounded Knee 12
Wratten, George 22

Y

Yale University 100
Yavapai Apache 45

Z

Ziyeh (wife) 68

ABOUT THE AUTHOR

Jon Sterngass is the author of *First Resorts: Pursuing Pleasure at Saratoga Springs, Newport, and Coney Island* (Johns Hopkins Univ. Press, 2001). He currently is a freelance writer specializing in children's nonfiction books. He has written more than 40 books; his most recent work is a biography of John Brown and an analysis of the steroids controversy in the United States. Born and raised in Brooklyn, Jon Sterngass has a BA in history from Franklin and Marshall College, an MA from the University of Wisconsin-Milwaukee in medieval history, and a PhD from City University of New York in nineteenth-century American history. He has lived in Saratoga Springs, New York, for 16 years with his wife, Karen Weltman, and sons Eli (16) and Aaron (13). As a child, he rooted for Cochise in the movie *Broken Arrow* and cried when he read about the death of Mangas Coloradas. In that sense, writing a biography of Geronimo brings him full circle.